This is the first book in the Love Cycle by David Loye. Books in this cycle are: *3,000 Years of Love. 100 Days of Love. 1001 Days of Love.* Also *Darwin on Love*—and *Darwin in Love!* See the back pages of this book and the website for The Benjamin Franklin Press for publication dates and availability through internet book sellers and bookstores globally.

If you like this book, please tell your friends and consider it for a gift to that special person or persons in your life for Christmas, New Years, birthdays, anniversaries, or for other special occasions.

Benjamin Franklin
benfranklin@benjaminfranklinpress
www.benjaminfranklinpress.com

3000 Years of Love

By the author

The Healing of a Nation
The Leadership Passion
The Knowable Future
The Sphinx and the Rainbow
The Partnership Way (with Riane Eisler)
An Arrow Through Chaos
Darwin's Lost Theory of Love
The Story of a Family
The Evolutionary Outrider, Editor
The Great Adventure, Editor
Bankrolling Evolution
Measuring Evolution
Brave Laughter
Return to Amalfi
Darwin's Lost Theory
Darwin on Love

3,000 YEARS OF LOVE

DAVID LOYE

Benjamin Franklin Press
First Edition

Published by
The Benjamin Franklin Press
A BFPress First Edition

1. Biography.   2. Social activism.   3. Poetry.

Cover painting by Barbara Schaefer, design by John Mason. Production: Cassandra Gallup-Bridge.
Back cover photo: Cathleen Roundtree.

For more information about Benjamin Franklin Press books
www.benjaminfranklinpress.com
benfranklin@benjaminfranklinpress.com
The Benjamin Franklin Press, P.O. Box 222851, Carmel, CA 93923
Phone: 831-624-6027. Fax: 831-626-3734

Copyright © 2007 David Loye
All rights reserved.
ISBN-13: 978-0-9789827-5-1
ISBN-10: 0-9789827-5-4

Dedicated to Riane
and to our children and our grandchildren
of the body, mind, and soul.

CONTENTS

PROLOGUE		1
ONE	HOW WE ALMOST DIDN'T MEET	3
TWO	THE FATEFUL PHONE CALL	6
THREE.	AT LAST WE MEET	8
FOUR	100 DAYS OF LOVE	12
FIVE	EARLY POEMS	16
SIX	THE HIDDEN MAVEN	22
SEVEN	THE DARK VISITOR	28
EIGHT	OFF TO THE NEW LIFE	35
NINE	RIANE'S EARLIER LIFE	48
TEN	MY EARLY LIFE	60

ELEVEN	ITALY, UNCLE MAIER, AND THE GLACIER AND THE FLAME	71
TWELVE	RIANE'S BOOKS	79
THIRTEEN	THE WOMEN'S MOVEMENT AND AFRICA	89
FOURTEEN	OF THE HYDRA AND GREECE	105
FIFTEEN	THE GERG ADVENTURE	115
SIXTEEN	MY BOOKS	125
SEVENTEEN	OUR THEORIES	135
EIGHTEEN	THE PARTNERSHIP ADVENTURE	148
NINETEEN	GERMANY, REGRESSION, AND THE PUSH TO A BETTER WORLD	161
TWENTY	THE MARCH ON MOSCOW AND MARRIAGE	178

TWENTY-ONE	WHO AM I?	186
TWENTY-TWO	THE DARK VISITOR RETURNS	193
TWENTY-THREE	WHO ARE WE, AND WHERE ARE WE GOING?	203
TWENTY-FOUR	MORE POEMS	211
TWENTY-FIVE	GOODBYE SOMETIME	217
TWENTY-SIX	3,000 YEARS OF LOVE	230
EPILOGUE		240
ABOUT OUR BOOKS		245
ABOUT OUR COVER		246
ABOUT THE AUTHOR		247
BENJAMIN FRANKLIN PRESS BOOKS 2007-2009		251

PROLOGUE

In this book I have brought together a private and a public story within the larger story of the lives of all of us.

Some may say that, as convention dictates, I should have kept the three stories properly apart. I can only answer that love in its actuality, rather than the pale mirroring usually allowed us, knows no such boundaries. And surely, if ever stories of love across the boundaries that shut us off from one another are needed, it is in our world today.

The time of this adventure story—for this is what it became—is roughly from the 1970s into the 21st century in America and the larger world.

These were the years during which worldwide many of us went from great hope to great disappointment and apprehension. From by and large welcoming to fearing the future. From a time for most of us of an acceptable "normality" to a new state of threat to ourselves and our planet.

On discovering each other, this was the world that Riane and I were delirious with joy to put aside. To skip the newspaper at breakfast and get on into another glorious day. To breathe freely. To just live and be.

And then we found the greater love and the greater joy. We found the best of all lives in the meld of our love for each other, and of ours together for what I am convinced the majority of us now living on this

David Loye

earth cherish and value and want to see prevail everywhere.

We found the joy of confronting all that works against this vision. We found our larger home and the hope that refuses to be put down or beat down, in together as scientists and as writers fighting for this vision of what can be, should be, and must be.

For the word was meant to sing and dance and inspire us to fulfill ourselves, not to lie flat and dead on the page. And love was meant for the world, not only for oneself and one other alone.

And as a link in the chain of being on and on into the future, laughter not sorrow must be our destiny.

ONE
HOW WE ALMOST DIDN'T MEET

I am now 82, looking back at that early time. Ah, how it was then!

So driven by joy was I that all I had to do to write a poem a day for our first three months together was to find and form the first line in my head—and the rest rolled out like a child released from school for summer vacation or a colt to the open pasture.

As for our love, what can I say? She was 46, I was 52. We had both had first marriages, mine for 25 years, hers for 15 years. We had children, two for her, four for me.

There were of course the many positives that come back to one now as well as the negatives overwhelming then, but we had both come to despair of finding the right partner during this lifetime. Reluctantly but realistically, I was prepared to accept the fact I was fated to live on as essentially only half a person with the rest of me missing somewhere out there beyond this lifetime.

And then it happened.

I was at the time a research psychologist attached to the Neuropsychiatric Institute of the UCLA School of Medicine. I had left Princeton to become the research director for what, over seven years, became a pioneering half-million-dollar study of the impact of movies and television on adults. My office was off campus in Westwood

David Loye

Village.

As so many do, thousands I'm sure, I had left the East coast with my wife and four children hoping that with the change of scene my troubled marriage would settle down and work out. But it hadn't. Shortly after our move I left my wife again and was dragging through what I was finding, to my astonishment, to be both the frightening and deadly process of dating other women.

Here I was in the capital of the movie stars and those aspiring to be stars. Hollywood was near by. All about me were the slim and nubile young blondes on campus, or lolling in the sun in sidewalk cafes, or waving gaily from open sports cars. On all sides were women of the beauty of one's dreams. And yet between me and them I had discovered there was an impassable gulf.

After the settled verities of twenty-five years of marriage, I was discovering the unbelievable, and yet I have since heard it from others—that Los Angeles could be the loneliest of all cities. And when I did bridge the gap, with a brief exception here and there, the experience again and again seemed flat and dead-ended.

There was a woman in my office who was typing the manuscripts of the books I was writing in those days, Elizabeth Dolmat. One day, on seeing me drag in from another dead ended foray into the rhinestone desert, she spoke up brightly.

"You know, I know just the woman for you."

"Yes?"

"She's very pretty and she's also writing a book. I'm typing her manuscript, too. She's very smart. She's interested in the future and likes classical music and good art."

I was becoming quite interested.

"She's in her mid-forties, I would say."

This was beginning to sound very good, for I had come to think this was probably the right age for me.

"She's an attorney."

This was still fine, this could be interesting.

"As a matter of fact, she's a divorce attorney."

Alas, the warning bell rang. For I was slowly facing up to the fact that this was where I was headed in my marriage and just mentioning the word was enough to me to signal monumental problems.

"Her name is Riane Eisler."

That did it. Something about the harsh sound of "Eisler" locked the image firmly in place. A divorce attorney no doubt cold and hard as nails. And Eisler? All I could think of was the equally harsh sound of . . . what was it? Eichman! Adolf Eichman, the heinous Nazi killer of the Jews! Adolf Eichman's female counterpart now a divorce attorney, hard as nails.

So the mind works in its strange, strange ways.

"Oh, she sounds delightful. I will have to look her up," I said to Elizabeth Dolmat not wanting to disappoint her. Privately, however, I told myself I would fry in hell before I went near that one.

TWO
THE FATEFUL PHONE CALL

A whole year passed. A year in which she might have gone one way, I another. One of us could have died. Or become locked into another relationship. Or married another, never to meet.

A whole year with repeat after repeat for this dismal little drama. I would drag in from another date. Elizabeth Dolmat would say, "You really should call Riane Eisler. You two are made for each other."

"Oh yes," I would say, "so glad you mentioned her. I really must," I would say once again privately knowing hell would freeze over before I would weaken and be driven to the arms of such a monster.

Then one day the phone rang. The voice asked for Elizabeth.

It was an incredible voice, with a touch of an accent, what was it? British? Latin? All I knew was that it summoned wonder to mind and seemed to wrap itself around my soul.

"No, Elizabeth isn't here," I said. "But *who* shall I say called."

"Riane Eisler," the voice said.

It couldn't be. It was impossible. I had never met her, she existed only as the most looney of fictions in my mind. Yet in the way we stereotype with so little to go on, what my mind fed to me was the immediate assurance that this was *not* the Riane Eisler I knew so well.

Still there was this voice.

3,000 Years of Love

For Homer, it was the sirens who lured Ulysses and his men ashore. For Heine, it was the Lorelei who enticed men to drown in the Danube. For Keats, it was the Belle Dame Sans Merci, the love of whom had wrecked many a man. Over and over again the story had been the same—of the heartless monster with the enticing body and the most seductive of voices.

Could this be a case of that nemesis for men that poets over the centuries had written of?

The contradiction must be resolved, the mystery ended. So I kept her on the line talking, talking, talking, until everything dissolved but that the two of us must now meet as soon as possible on the pretext of talking about anything but what was actually in our minds.

THREE
AT LAST WE MEET

How can I describe that voice as I first heard it?

It was a voice, but yet more than a voice. There was something about it like a new and enticing aroma or exotic scene from elsewhere. There was about it a sense of the tropics, of palm trees, of sultry nights.

But no, that wasn't quite it, for there was also about it something of a European elegance—and yet also something of the restraint and concern for the proprieties of a British precision. I was confused but also entranced.

That first phone contact was on a Thursday. We were to meet for lunch at her house the following Saturday.

Over the intervening days my mind roamed the exotic possibilities of what the woman behind the voice would look like. The sultry undertone suggested the ample blonde of the movies. After all, Hollywood itself was only a few miles on to the East from Westwood Village.

The more elegant European overlay, however, suggested a trim figure, still voluptuous but more restrained. No doubt with compelling eyes.

As for the touch of a British accent, this brought to mind beauty ranging from the pert and long-lashed sparkle of Vivienne Leigh to the wry, bustling, and direct appeal of Katherine Hepburn.

But now the day itself was here. As I approached the door bell, I began to fear the worst. A succession of monstrous images out of Hieronymous Bosch assailed me. I rang the bell and waited. And waited. And waited. Then with a creak, the door opened a crack. A short and muscular Latino woman peered up at me, her face crumpled into a grimace of extreme reluctance if not active repugnance.

As if my arrival had given her a sudden stomach ache, she eyed me, saying nothing. It was not a promising beginning. Perhaps the whole thing was a mistake.

I asked for the name I was to come to know so well. Nothing happened.

I explained I was expected, providing my own name.

Reluctantly, still wordless, this fierce guardian, this Cerberus at the gate as in some legend, I suppose one might say, then stood aside just enough to allow me to squeeze past her And so I was inside wondering what next.

As if with an unseen puff of smoke, the woman who went with the voice appeared.

Had she been waiting nearby? Watching perhaps from behind a wall or pillar from which, unseen, she could see who entered?

Had she been similarly wondering if what went with my voice was up to expectations? Wondering if I would be too short? Too fat? Too gross, who knows? On finding me acceptable, had she now emerged, as if by chance, casually?

She was both not at all and at the same time exactly what I had expected. She was tall, slim, and indeed elegant. At the same time there was about her an aura of down-to-earth, workaday practicality. There was a merry light in her grey-blue eyes. There was an intriguing tilt to her nose and overall an impish look both to her face and her full lipped smile. Her hair was dark brown and curly, shaped close to her head but somewhat more ample than what one might call a boyish cut. She was clad in jeans that were both the fashion and the practical working clothes of the day.

These jeans, I noticed as I followed her into the living room, were well-selected to show off her trim figure, with a casual blouse asserting the ample fullness of her breasts. She was indeed a beauty. When later I came to know she had been born and been a child in Vienna before the devastation of Hitler and the Nazis, I saw that in looks she could have been a younger sister to the actress Hedy Lamar, who I think had come from Vienna and was also Jewish. But it was her smile that served to punctuate and most swiftly establish the power of her presence over one.

It was a smile that, like a flower whose unfolding had been caught in stop motion photography, quietly exploded. It was a smile that like the fireworks in the night caught and held you for the entrancing moment. All at once saucy, warm, gracious and full, it was a smile conveying what seemed both a deep knowledge of and a liking for you.

I know this must sound exaggerated way out of proportion, but it is true to both what I saw and what I felt.

I followed her about the house as in a trance. I found myself chattering like a magpie, as they say, in a rush to tell her everything about myself that might possibly intrigue and win her. But she, too, was chattering in the same way I can see now looking back, also seeking to make sure of me.

She came to my apartment that evening for dinner, returned to her home at the properly discrete hour for what might or might not be classified as a "first date."

Then at 2:00 in the morning I woke to the flutter of an impulse. Would the words come that I wanted?

Slowly at first and then swiftly the first line formed and I began to write. Within minutes it was there—slight, but not bad, I thought.

> Who are you?
> Something in you
> seems to speak to
> me out of a past
> beyond remembering,
> or from a future
> too far ahead
> to yet behold.
> Who are you with
> the elfin smile
> and soft hands?
> Why do I love you
> so intensely
> so quickly?

I dressed and drove the bright and lonely streets back across Los Angeles to her home to drop this first poem in the mail slot in her front door.

The next day, and the next, and the next, as poem after poem flowed from me, this became a new ritual of delight for my life.

FOUR
100 DAYS OF LOVE

By now I sense the feeling we get when people are too much in love with love and with themselves in public. At first it is charming; our hearts are touched. But if beyond a certain point it's prolonged it becomes cloying, then annoying, then one just wants to go elsewhere to get away from it.

Who are these insufferably self-centered people in a world that cries out for awareness of all the rest of us—for the reality of our lives, and hopes, and fears? Who are these people who do not properly draw the curtains, or seem to go to work, or stick to what's properly fretful and properly meaningful in our workaday lives?

To most of us who value love it is a private thing that loses its value under public display. I think of the story in the Oklahoma of my youth of Mrs.Skelly, wife of the oilman of that name who made it big with Skelly Oil. They told of how she opened her palatial home to display all her clothes and jewels in glass cases, with a track of red carpet and velvet ropes to allow the people of Tulsa, the peons, the upper crust, anybody, to pour through on weekends to marvel at her possessions. Pretentious, jejune, some would say; others would say uppity.

This is the risk I've faced in telling this story. But how else could it be? One has to have a starting point and this was it for us.

God knows, as we used to say, or simply the fact of life tells us that the roller coaster of all that is properly serious, and challenging, exhilerating, dismaying, frightening, and just plain awful lay behind and still lay ahead for us—and for this book. But we *deserved* this bright break in the journey. This casting off the existential loneliness, this lift of vision of a better world.

As others we have known and still know *deserved* and *deserve* it. As indeed there is not a single soul living on this earth who at birth does not deserve it!

For don't all of us—some more than others, but in one way or another, after 100,000 years still all of us—come to love out of a world in which love is so often the stranger standing with the tin cup on the corner, or a sign saying "Homeless, will work for food" in an alien land.

And about this matter of, God help us, poems!

The cynic will sniff at, or the sophisticate of today trivialize, the impulse to write love poems as "naive," "passe," "old hat," or whatever else may be useful for the old game of the put down for feeling or spontaneity. But I knew then and ever since have been grateful to have had the gift and the drive to record what remains universal—this lift, this soaring wonderment in love's earliest days that is everyone's who has ever loved.

I am particularly grateful now, as our years together draw toward their inevitable close, that what I set down then is still here to swiftly bring it all back to me.

Old photos or old letters may suffice for some. All too many of us, however, pass through this life without even that to take from the trunk or box or chest, and to look at, or to read, and thereby deepen one's sense of what is meaningful about life.

In defiance of the emotional and verbal poverty of our impaired and diminished age, I am grateful for having reveled in what has lifted hearts and minds in all ages. For through these poems I may now live a double life—then and now, then and now, then and now, as in the tolling of a joyous bell to herald the morning.

I suppose they might eventually have died in an old trunk somewhere had they not by accident been hooked to my addiction with writing for publication.

"I really love your poems," she said to me one day after I had been writing them daily for about two weeks. "You know they are so good that I think if you go on writing them they could become a book."

This struck me as a very interesting idea. Coming back to writing poetry after thirty years of journalism and science and a seemingly endless stream of prose either for pay or imprisoned by the stuffy constraints of scientific writing, I had discovered the wonderful freedom of this new voice. Along with this new love itself, it was like not only being young again, but ageless.

Yes, that was it, so wondrous, intriguing, and immortal about what I felt in writing these poems. It was as if somehow impossibly, but now most certainly, life, along with love, might go on, and on, and on.

"In fact," she said, "if you can go on writing them, I have thought of a wonderful title for a book."

"Oh yes," I said with mounting interest, "what is it?"

"100 Days of Love," she said.

"100 Days of Love. Yes," I said, "that's a wonderful title!"

But then it hit me.

"But this would mean I would have to turn out these poems one a day for more than three months," I said.

"Yes, I know," she said. A mischievous smile worked across her lips as she eyed me. "But you could do it—if you really love me."

Was she serious? I stared at her. It was hard to tell. The smile told me she was just being playful. But there was a look in her eye that seemed to mean business. I didn't know her well enough yet to be sure.

"Well, of course I love you...," I said, wondering how to back out gracefully—or, crazily, impossibly, go ahead.

On one hand I knew that of course, rusty as I was by then at this sort of thing, daily immersed in statistics and research design, it would likely be easier for me to fly to the moon than to write a love poem a day for 100 days. I knew she really wouldn't hold me to it.

But on the other hand there was the uncomfortable pull of the archetype for the old fairy tale. I saw that happenstance, fate, whatever it was, had plunked me down into the old story of the prince who must fight the dragon. Or climb the mountain through the ring of fire. Or answer the runic riddle that has sunk a thousand previous suitors. Or pass some other impossible task to win the fair one.

Filled as my childhood had been with these tales—which have sustained far more of us than realize it through many a dark day and hour—the outcome was inescapable. I was hooked and must make the best of it.

And so I did. My daily poems became the book that later led to the fact and title of this book.

FIVE
EARLY POEMS

The next four poems I wrote surprised and delighted both of us. For me they took me back to when I was nineteen, in the Navy in World War II, and had signed a contract with Farrar & Rinehart to publish both my first novel and first book of poetry.

Neither were ever accepted or published. Nor were those that followed. So I gave up serious writing in my early thirties to knuckle down to journalism, public relations, and anything else that would keep a roof over our heads, food in our mouths, and clothes and all else for the long, still meaningful early life with my first wife and our four children.

As for Riane, I can only, with I should think good reason, guess that to her these poems must have pointed to the future rather than the past. Promising tokens of the possibility this time it might last, might even be that wan hope that reason always rejects as impossible, be forever.

3,000 Years of Love

Second Poem

My world was empty rich
until I met you.
It had the fullness
I clasped and danced to,
yet all was ultimately hollow.
It was the merry-go-round
without the music.
It was the birthday cake
without the buried silver dollar.
Now rocketing I cannot
cover, or hope to cover
in a lifetime this strange
new double world.
this new sun, new moon, new stars—
this new and endless horizon.

David Loye

Third Poem

Our love is a
merry creature.
Beyond the sound
of trumpets and the
roar of water falls,
that is its charm.
It can laugh at itself—
like an elf, or new-to-this-
earth-hand-clapping child.

Fourth Poem

The old saw about
heartache is true.
'Twas no word for me
until I met you.
Now even the smallest
parting brings it on.
It'll become familiar
before this tale is done.

David Loye

Fifth Poem

Oh I have known love
before, its golden
possession is no mystery.
But this is something
new, for which I
have no name.
I shall call it this
thing that is like a
river meandering
through green meadows,
from which deer drink
in which swim fish
of shapes and colors
never seen before.
A river with rapids,
falls, long placid stretches
under the sun, the eyes
closed, sun upon the
eyes, the raft drifting,
but no shoals.
A river called by its
Indian fishermen, "The
River of Two Headwaters."

3,000 Years of Love

And then ahead, unknown then but foreshadowing so much that later came to be, was poem fifty eight.

> The prevalence of visions
> is no accident.
> If the capacity for
> peak experiences is
> characteristic of self-actualizers
> then it follows that the
> marriage of two such
> creatures should result in
> shared and multiple peaks.
> And so last night Janss
> steps were transfigured, you
> and I at the top, the bright
> panoply of playing field and
> building lights ahead, the
> flow of people as though in
> a movie around us down the
> long steps, the embrace of
> trees like warm wings to
> either side and all afloat,
> as though it were all our
> own great space ship moving
> with an incredible majesty
> toward the distant moon
> and its lone star.

SIX
THE HIDDEN MAVEN

We had known each other for about a month when one day something happened I came to learn has happened to many others. For a time, it had dropped out of memory as not making any sense, but then there returned to me, in a flashback, a startling image from six months earlier.

Feeling particularly lonely, despairing of ever finding the right woman, I had been in my car driving through Westwood Village when suddenly there appeared directly ahead of me, hovering beyond the windshield, a picture of a woman.

Solely as a phenomenon, this is not unusual. Such pictures appear, as if forming in the air, to many of us all the time in daydreams. We tend to forget this happened as they become a seamless aspect of our consciousness.

As James Thurber parodied in what became the Danny Kaye movie "The Secret Life of Walter Mitty," to a far greater extent than we realize we daily float in and out between fantasy and reality.

This particular Mitty picture that floated there before me, just beyond the windshield, was something that had come out of all the months, which seemed by then years, of looking for my hypothetical missing other half. It came as though in answer to a desperate unspoken query, "Who is she? What does she look like?"

There had suddenly appeared the picture of an attractive woman in her mid forties, with curly brown hair cropped close to her head, with a tilt to the nose, eyes made larger and brighter by the thick lenses of the horn-rimmed glasses Riane sometimes wore, sporting an impish smile.

It was Riane I had seen! Exactly as she did look—and this was six months before I met her.

A second incident of this kind occurred five days after we met. Before moving to Los Angeles and the UCLA School of Medicine, I had known little of so-called psychic phenomena—other than it was not something to indulge in if you were career minded. But the dumping of psychologist Thelma Moss from the faculty for the heresy of daring to investigate methods of so-called psychic diagnosis and healing had outraged me. I decided to sit in on a session of a forlorn little research group Moss had left behind. They were studying telepathy, or both short and long distance accurate transmission of information by means unknown. Soon, intrigued by what I saw work with my own eyes, I agreed to become the faculty sponsor for the little group.

Officially listing our sessions as "research on mind-brain interaction" to avoid the heavy hand of the fearful "powers that be," we met every Wednesday evening in a room in the basement of the Neuropsychiatric Institute.

The investigation was of special interest not only to me but also to a widening number of open-minded and venturesome doctors elsewhere. Concern was mounting about the astronomical rising cost of the new CAT scans and other exotic machines for medical diagnosis. What if there really *was* something to the idea, generally contemptuously rejected, of the skills claimed by psychics for "reading" the nature of a person's illness? If psychic diagnosis could be pinned down and verified, this could offer vast economies in a time of dangerously rising medical costs.

And what if there really was something to the claims of so-called psychic healers? What if this should prove to be a quality possessed by many doctors, but not by others, which could be reliably identified? Wouldn't there be the potential for tremendous savings in dollars and malpractice suits?

Most importantly, it could mean a considerable reduction in pain and agony for patients who were not only misdiagnosed but were being ostensibly treated by so-called healers who had no more real capacity for healing than an old refrigerator.

The leader of the research group was a young man, Barry Taff, who looked like a smaller version of the Martian with pointed ears and frozen face of Star Trek fame, "Mr.Spock." A consultant to movie makers on films about the paranormal, Barry had the reputation of being a gifted psychic diagnostician. To try to probe how psychic diagnosis might work, the group was involved in an ongoing experiment to test the degree to which telepathy—or "reading another's mind"—was a so-called natural gift that could be trained through practice, as one might teach a child to read.

The procedure involved having everybody sit in a circle of chairs, facing each other. One person was chosen at random to act as the "target" upon whom the others were to focus. Taff would then lull everyone into a light trance with the usual soothing talk for inducing relaxation from head to toe, the target person would say the name of someone they knew, then everybody else would focus on this name and report whatever images came floating into their minds.

The results were often uncanny. Here was someone far off and wholly unknown to all of us in the room except by a first name reported by someone who likewise was generally a complete stranger. And yet out of the images reported by the rest of us focusing on this name often it was confirmed by the "target" person that anywhere from a significant number to a clear majority of these images actually fit the person they were thinking of.

In other words, out of the images would emerge a composite picture of what this unknown person looked like, their favorite clothes, their occupations, even what their ailments or medical problems were.

This was exciting to me because it revealed that the capacity for telepathy, and thereby so-called psychic diagnosis, was not only widely available in people who had no idea they had some degree of this ability, but that it was also a capacity that actually could be trained.

And so back to Riane. I had first met her on a Saturday—thus this was the first time I had any idea of what she looked like, let alone that there might in the future be any significant connection for us. On Sunday, finding her to be skeptical but also curious about this fascinating experiment and its results, I invited her to sit in with the group on the following Wednesday night. At the refreshment break for the group midway through the evening's session, a woman came up to the two of us.

"Do you mind if I interrupt?" she said.

"No, go ahead," I said.

"Do you remember me? I was here last week."

Except for a core of regular experimenters, each week the participants differed except for a few volunteers who would also return for another session out of curiosity.

"Yes, I remember you," I said.

"I was sitting directly across from you," she said, "and looking at you I thought to myself 'that man looks so lonely.'"

Then her face brightened and in wonder she looked first at me and then at Riane.

"And at that moment," she said, "suddenly I saw *you*" – she pointed to Riane – "sitting right beside him!"

I was at first puzzled, then thunderstruck. As these sessions were for training telepathy, the woman assumed that Riane was someone known to me at the time and no doubt close, a wife or lover, perhaps back home at the time.

Yet at the time she had in mind seen Riane sitting next to me not only did I have no idea through actual contact of what Riane looked like, I hadn't even spoken to her yet—for the phone call that first connected us came the next day after the Wednesday session of the preceding week.

What the woman was reporting was clearly a case of precognition—or seeing in advance what comes to be in the future.

Skeptics, understandably, have great difficulty with this sort of thing. Indeed, I have found that in our culture and at this point in our evolution, it is almost impossible to believe this happens unless one is either very gullible or, as a research scientist or otherwise, has personally experienced this subterranean linking of ourselves to one another and to all of nature.

It is an area of research laden with polemics and by now mountains of technicalities of language and method in science. I have, as a scientist, written two reasonably popular books, *The Sphinx and the Rainbow* and *An Arrow Through Chaos,* to try to explain how this happens. Still it remains best captured in the metaphors of personal experience. Here I have found the image of plunging into deep water useful.

3,000 Years of Love

It is as though most of the time we are swimming near shore, in shallow water through which we can see the sandy bottom not far beneath us. But then through a plunge beneath the surface we find ourselves in a region of deeper currents, of channels unseen from the surface, in a below surface world of passages through underwater caverns only dimly glimpsed—of laws, we might say, interconnecting us in a way beyond what our minds can grasp, but which the fearless heart knows and follows without the language yet to understand.

One constant I have found is that strong emotion, either positive or negative, most reliably seems to seek out and forge the link in these hidden chains of interconnection that can bind us to one another. Thus while hate can undermine love, and I am now convinced at the extreme can even destroy another, love—as I came to know it—actually lifts and binds us and can even heal.

I write of this now because I am no gullible tyro, but rather because as both lover and scientist I have over many years probed love seeking to understand its mysteries.

I write of it because I know that many a reader thinking back will confirm this from their own experience—that there is this about that special love, or special time in the course of a lesser love: that there comes the time when something seems to swirl up and embrace the two of you out of both the past and the future in a way I am sure will take us at least another century or two—assuming we have them—to begin to understand.

SEVEN
THE DARK VISITOR

So it was—this world that was ours, this by no means lost world I want to bring back to life here because of how badly we need anything that can tell us of what love is, was, contends with, tries to heal, or transcends.

And then it came rolling into our lives—like a gust of cold wind around the dirty, dusty corner of the bleak city as the door to your home closes behind you and you confront the winter world, like the first touch of chill off the plain in winter.

I see now she was fearful I would leave her on discovering it. For it was no minor thing.

It is not of course that I was shallow, or that she thought I was shallow. But there was the practical side to it. For given any other alternative, what man on short acquaintance would want to be saddled with the inconvenience of a sickly and potentially seriously ill person suddenly on their hands?

At first, it slowly edged toward my consciousness, avoiding the full awareness. But from the outset I see now there slowly rose and tugged within us a recognition of the horror it would be to become so deeply, irreparably in love as we soon came to see we were, and then to find ourselves—for this too we did feel, however irrational—separated by her death.

It was not a completely irrational conclusion. We both were old enough to see or hear of our own contemporaries beginning to die. The friend who one day was healthy and happy and the next day dead of a heart attack. Or, even worse, the friend who over a year went slowly from radiant beauty to a walking skeleton literally being eaten alive by cancer.

There was also in both of us the fear that at last having gained in each other what all our lives we had been hungering for, now it was to be snatched back and forever denied us—for this, we both knew, was all too often the way of the world.

It was this fear I can see now she had that I would bow out on discovering the truth. As long as she could, she hid it. But what was the truth?

I had come to know of her collapse and that supposedly she was now recovering. But what was still wrong with her? One day while we were walking she suddenly gasped and clutched at her chest from the exertion of merely trying to climb a slight incline. Ruefully, she revealed she was going to one of the best heart specialists in Beverly Hills to try to find out what the trouble was. Her mother had died suddenly, without warning, of a heart defect. She feared she might face the same fate.

Soon I found the same chest pains came on whenever either one of us lost our temper and raged at the other—for rage we did, and still do, as I would guess all people of passionate convictions and a hard won personal integrity must sometimes.

One quickly gets over it if sustained by the love that is prepared to quickly apologize or do whatever else is necessary for reassurance. But with her there was no buffer—she seemed to have been stripped of her natural defenses. While I was protected from her rage by healthy defenses built up over many years, my rage against her, or even anger, could be devastating.

I found she was also suffering almost constant lower back pains, with her back often "going out" with excruciating pain. I accompanied her on her regular visits to a prominent Westwood Village back specialist. I watched in horror as he jabbed the muscles in her lower back with a hypodermic needle that looked like the size of something one would use with a horse or elephant. The needle, he explained, was filled with glucose that would harden the muscles, which were too slack, allowing her back to "go out."

He had written a published book with his picture on the cover and seemed to have a good reputation. But I felt there was something radically wrong with the approach and was relieved to find her gradually dropping the visits.

There were the stomach pains that assailed her practically every night, forcing her to writhe in agony and go without sleep sometimes for hours. For this, rather than just prescribing another pill, Dr.Ford, a wonderful old general practitioner she was going to, had a practical suggestion. He explained that because of her often high state of anxiety, she was quite likely swallowing a lot of air. This, like an inflated balloon, pressed upon the walls of her stomach causing pain. She was to stop talking during meals and sip all liquids through a straw rather than gulping them down.

For a time this seemed to help, but then gradually the problem returned.

Additionally, there was the hour a week with a woman I came to know to be an excellent counselor. This I knew to be enormously helpful, but I could see she had so much to contend with working within her that this, too, was uphill going all the way. To top it off, whenever she seemed for a while to be in reasonably good shape, the inflamation known as conjunctivitis would attack her eyes.

Soon I came to see that neither she nor her doctors, nor those who had preceded them, knew what was the truth of the matter.

One might guess, but no one knew for sure the cause, or what the cure might be, or whether there was a cure. Or even—although the focus was all on her recovery, and the assumption was that she would recover, the question that now haunted me, as I see in retrospect it haunted her as well—how long in fact did she have to live?

Was it to be five years? Ten years? Twenty? Or only another year or two, or even six months? Or less?

> All evening the shadow
> hovered, oh my dear I
> cannot bear these fears
> that having barely possessed
> you now you could be
> taken from me by the
> Great Gross Sportsman—
> that burly being
> who so blithely guns
> down and bags here
> all that is lovely,
> noble, delicate,
> rare, and endangered.
> My love must be your
> escape, your shelter,
> your mountainous and
> deep woods hideaway.
>
> (continued)

David Loye

> I hear his fat footstep near,
> the cock of the gun, the
> coo of the lips and the
> lure of the teasing whistle
> as your sweet life through
> too much pain, joy, or
> disorder shatters.
> I hear and will again
> and again and again
> bar the door.

There settled into me the sense of a mission that has been with me ever since. I was in love with her, yes of course, and I wanted to see our love go on and on. But there was more to it.

At the core of this sense of mission I see now were two things at work. Reflected by the fact of my own training and professional attachment to the Neuropsychiatric Institute and the school of medicine, at the time I saw that I was in a unique position to pull together the pieces of a complex picture psychologically as well as physically in a way that might help her fully regain her health. But I was also in a unique position to comprehend a larger dimension beyond our love and hopes for a long life together.

Though before I knew her—and ever since, over the long years we have been together—others have glimpsed this in her, and loved her and have tried to help her, I believe I was the first person to fully comprehend the potential within her for the important contribution she was to make.

I know to some this will sound impossibly pretentious. Put on. Exaggerated for effect. But for me it was a simple existential fact. I will never stray from this conviction. In the unpublished writings she had shown me, in the unusual quality of her mind, and in what I came to see was her passionate drive to make ours a better world, I had glimpsed what could, and indeed did prove, to be her contribution.

I would say that more than merely a matter of intuition or emotion on my part, this was a mystical experience. For as I know has happened with others, there began to nudge at me the feeling we had not simply been brought together coincidentally. Increasingly, I felt I had been brought into her life for a purpose and with a mission, and that mission was to protect her from all that roamed loose throughout our world looking for such as her to suppress and do away with.

I decided to set aside my attempts to find grants to extend my own research, and even my own writing, and devote my time mainly to this mission. I went with her during appointments with health care providers trying to work on one or another aspect of the problem. I queried them about what they were doing and the hoped for outcomes. I examined the records for her past health care involvements with heart specialists, osteopaths, gynecologists, and the practitioners of so-called alternative medicine, then just getting underway.

Other than an experience I will come to, she had received the most meaningful help from an old man well known in alternative medicine then, Dr. Henry Beiler, the author of the ground-breaking *Food is Your Best Medicine*.

Then a man in his eighties, Dr. Beiler was so captivated by this special quality that I and others found in her, he had driven up from his office in San Juan Capistrano, some fifty miles south of Los Angeles, to care for her during her collapse. Terminating her normal diet of practically everything that was bad for her, he had put her on a strict regime of organic health foods—including the famous Beiler Soup, a horrendous concoction of green beans and zucchini—to which she attributed some unknown bit of the credit for recovery from the collapse. A little clay statuette of dancing bears he gave her still graces our living room coffee table.

EIGHT
OFF TO THE NEW LIFE

Looking back now, I can see that at the time America, as well as a good part of the world, was teetering on the brink of an abyss. There hung over the heads of every sentient being among us the nuclear bomb-tipped terror of the Iron Curtain impasse between East and West, pivotally hinging on the stand off between the U.S. and the Soviet Union. There was this great underlying uncertainty, the nagging drag on one's spirit, this gnawing question of what was going to happen and where on earth was it all headed.

But within the wonderful small new niche we'd found within the sigh and roll and the crunch and cries of the larger world, our own life together seemed to be settling down.

Poem twenty-six, which I particularly enjoy on coming back to it fresh after all these years, seems to capture a good sense of the time.

Of the many poets and writers I have admired over the years, it reminds me a bit of Mark Twain. Of a not-so-frosty Robert Frost, whom I once sat at the foot of and listened to in undergraduate years at Dartmouth. Or Riane and my wonderful good friend now, Raffi, the magnificent "children's troubadour."

In any case, it said much of the best of those days.

David Loye

Poem Twenty-six

We're settling in.
Yes mam, we knew
we liked the place when
we first saw it,
but you never know.
Things can happen, things
can get out of joint
and so on. You know.
Well, I hope to tell you
this is some place,
yessiree. Why, you
can sit right here
and see one hell of
a stretch of mountains.
And let me tell you
when it rains she's
tight as a drum.
It hasn't snowed yet,
but I can tell you
those double-pane windows
will hold in one hell
of a lot of heat.
And the fireplace—
isn't that something now?
You know what, that
flue was put in

(continued)

3,000 Years of Love

>by a master builder.
>No smoke back-tracks
>into the room here.
>You put in your log
>and whooey in no
>time, let me tell
>you, mister, you got
>heat like nobody's business.
>Yes mam, and when the
>wind blows gentle of an
>evening, why this house
>plain hums like a
>fiddle box, like it
>was musical. Yes sir,
>we got everything we
>want here. I can tell
>you for sure, we're
>settled in for life.

How ironic in retrospect. For within far less time than either she or I could have guessed, the house in Westwood Village that inspired several of my early poems was a thing of the past.

I see now she had kept going for years by deep down denying there was anything seriously wrong with her until her collapse. Afterwards, in order to rebuild herself, she reverted to the same fierce denial. Again and again I was to see other evidence of a steel will that kept her going when others would give up or give in. But something about our new life together—that out of years of uncertainty she was now reasonably sure of a love that might last, that might even be strong enough to win a future for the two of us—melted the steel of both resolve and denial.

David Loye

She came to see the reality of what I perceived but out of consideration for her feelings could not talk of—that without a marked improvement in her health and an immense reduction in stress, she could not last many more years, however strong her basic constitution might be.

She began to talk of wanting to move elsewhere. As if fate sought to oblige us, the grant that had financed my move from Princeton to UCLA ran out, my job was ended, so I could go anywhere.

My own children were grown and gone—the oldest, my daughter Jenella in graduate school in entemology in Oklahoma, my daughter Kate an artist on her own now living with a boy friend, my son Chris finishing up in architecture at the University of Virginia, my son Jonathan off training for presumably the next war in the U.S. Army Rangers.

Riane's children—and there lay still another distressing story I did not understand until later—had troubling childhoods, for which Riane largely blamed herself. Her older daughter was much of the time away at boarding school in Arizona. Her younger daughter had finished high school and could go with us, but was reluctant to do so. But Riane felt she had to leave Los Angeles, that she could not heal without doing so.

It seemed to me at the time that it was the only sensible move, as it was becoming evident that the city held too many stressful memories, too many triggers to her recurring maladies. I also thought that her daughters too might be happier in a new place.

It was a time of large-scale social change as well. Little more than a year ahead lay the presidential election of Ronald Reagan and the radically new world we were moving into.

As that exceptionally well-grounded and sensible journalist Haynes

3,000 Years of Love

Johnson wrote in his book *Sleepwalking Through History,* immediately ahead lay "an age of illusions when America lived on borrowed time and squandered opportunities to put its house in order. Not since the laissez-faire years of the twenties had America experienced such a decade—and a decade that will extract a heavy price from Americans unborn. In their impact on social, economic, political/governmental life, and on the attitudes and personal values of Americans, the eighties were the most important years since World War II."

Johnson also chronicled "how the United States was transformed from world's leading creditor nation into the world's leading debtor, how its new debts mortgaged the nation's future, how the eighties ended with the greatest promise internationally in a half century and with a greater challenge for America to win the peace after the cold war," but also of "how the domestic and foreign policies of the eighties left America more vulnerable in the nineties to problems involving energy and hostage taking and relationships with terrorist third world states, how the most conservative administration of the century ended America's age of reform, how the American people and their leaders and political institutions appeared to be sleepwalking through history."

How "the nation traveled from the New Patriotism to the New Greed all within a mere decade," Johnson wrote back in 1991 of the prelude to the debacle that came to be our time.

Out in the California from which Reagan had come—indeed, bent on leaving the Hollywood that had provided his springboard to the presidency—we looked first to the south, to San Diego, then to the north, to Santa Barbara, but in neither place could we find something affordable Riane felt comfortable with.

We had decided perhaps it was best to give up looking for the time being when a pattern that was thereafter to be repeated often in our life took over.

Realizing how often and widely it must also seem to happen to others, the researcher in me says there is something here worth a study. It is this pattern of the appearance of someone at a critical point who seems to say the right thing, or points one in the right direction, as if they were, as in the old tales, a messenger of the gods—or in this case, the Goddess.

It is this feeling that our lives can not only form a story in the retelling, as here, but are at times shaped by the purpose of some larger story originally.

The one most meaningful place to me at UCLA was the Sunset Canyon swimming pool. This was a brilliant jewel of blue water, Olympic size, set in a high up grove of eucalyptus trees that hovered above Westwood Village like a friendly Sphinx.

My daily routine for years come lunchtime was to bolt down a nearby Taco Bell taco filled with chili, cheese, and lettuce, and then drive up into Sunset Canyon to swim and lie in the sun by the pool before returning to work for the afternoon. It had been a delight for me for weeks now to take Riane there, and to admire the sleek beauty of her body in a blue swimsuit as she dove into the pool or swam beside me.

The best experience of all was just to lie there on a beach towel together, and feeling the warmth of the earth beneath us and the warmth of the sun upon us, to look up into the eucalyptus trees overhead, to listen to the rustle of the leaves, and talk of the things that delighted us and of the life that lay ahead we planned together.

I wrote of one of those days in poem thirty-nine.

3,000 Years of Love

Poem Thirty-nine

Lying on our backs
we watched the tree
climb over us into the sky.
Beneath us the earth
at last was solid;
out from us there
zigzagged upward a crazy
symphony of branches and
twigs ringing the
firm, round, thrusting
trunk of our love.
There it was, our own
new life ascending
above us—oh that
smooth white probing of
budding vectors into the
deep blue pool of sky.

One day Riane came out of the women's bathhouse at the Sunset Canyon pool with an expression of both childlike wonder and delight on her face.

"I met a woman I know in there and told her about us, and how we wanted to leave Los Angeles, and she had an idea where we might go."

This, I was to learn, was typical. I tend to be a lone wolf, seldom asking advice of anybody when confronted with any kind of problem whatsoever. But she invariably asked for advice from everybody—indeed sometimes hordes of people it seemed to me—who came within her orbit, then sifted through this feedback to reach her decision.

"She said we should go to Carmel Valley," she reported.

And so we went there to see if this might be the Promised Land.

Carmel Valley we found extending inland from the seacoast just south of Monterey, California, about five hours drive north of Los Angeles and a 2 ½ hours drive south of San Francisco.

It was a beautiful valley of farms, horses, and vineyards intermingled with attractive but unpretentious homes. It was nestled in a wide sprawl of browned ranch land, with a string of green oases along a river, between two modest but still impressive mountain ranges that looked a bit like Switzerland to me. A delightful small village that looked somewhat like a Western movie village was about a half hour's drive out from the seacoast.

It seemed ideal to me and I thought the woman in the bathhouse must indeed have been a divine messenger. But Riane found the town of Carmel itself more attractive. Huddled along the coast between the outstretched arms of two wings of the Carmel bay, with the sea stretching on west all the way I suppose to Hawaii or Indonesia, it was like a wonderland out of a children's story book.

Tucked away along streets that wandered down into crevices then climbed sudden small hills was this town that everywhere summoned memories of one's favorite children's stories. Amid the gnarled and twisting branches of oaks were Hansel and Gretel houses such as Arthur Rackham once drew. Overall the charm, however, was most like that of the E.H.Shepherd drawings for Winnie the Pooh. The main streets were lined with interesting shops, and everywhere flowers were blooming—in the gardens of the homes, in the window boxes of the shops, in the multi-colored sprinkling of yellow, blue, red, and purple wild flowers along the seafront rim of what looked like it must surely be one of the most beautiful beaches on the coast.

"If this place is so good for flowers, it must be good for people," Riane said.

This seemed to settle it. We began looking for a house and soon found what looked to me like some delightful prospects within her price range—for the money involved would be hers, as I faced a divorce in which practically everything I owned including a house back east in Princeton would go to my wife. Riane, however, passed up the houses that caught my eye to settle on what seemed to me the absolute worst of all possibilities.

It was a grim, grey, cold and foggy day when we first saw it. The house in every way fit the weather. It was encased within what seemed to me a smothering and gloomy grove of California live oaks surrounded with what looked like a distinctly unfriendly high wall. The house itself was a sprawling, white stucco affair with many doors, which I found was extremely difficult to figure out and get around in. Nathaniel Hawthorne had written of the oppressive House of Seven Gables. Ringing the place with fitting confusion, this to me was the oppressive House of Seven Doors.

What had once been the front door was a massive carved wooden slab with iron hinges which seemed to me then could suitably have graced a prison. Containing a small window, through which one might see if a person knocking was to be let in or lose the dogs on, for some reason this door was no longer in use. One now entered through a door at the other end of the house into the kitchen, which was nearest the small parking area within the walls.

This kitchen was surely the most inauspicious entry point I had ever seen—later we were to find out this was one of the chief reasons the house had sat on the market for months unsold. The floor was covered with a worn, ancient sheet of battleship gray linoleum. The walls were plastered with a smoke-encrusted wallpaper of a patterned color that I privately identified to myself, with the accuracy of the eye of my teen years working on dairy farm, as "calf shit brown." The rest of the house on that dark day seemed hardly better.

"What did you think of it?" Riane asked as we left at a brisk pace, for I couldn't get away fast enough.

I could see that for some strange reason she was fairly dancing with delight and that this was an idea that needed to be scotched immediately.

"That is the most rundown, gloomy and horrible place I have ever seen," I said. "Did you see all those oaks? There must be thirty of them. I'm not getting any younger, you know. If I had to water all those oaks, I would be dead in two years!"

What I didn't know at the time was that you never water oaks. It's bad for them. As I later came to know, it can encourage the terrible yellow danger signal of oak root fungus. But also what I didn't know of was Riane's prior history of a canny eye for bargains in real estate and experience in remodeling and interior decorating.

For a while when her father was ill, she had taken over the management of the construction company he started in Los Angeles with the money from the sale of an alligator goods factory he built up in Cuba after their escape from Nazi Austria.

She also had behind her an experience with her father that mirrored what she now encountered with me. When she left her first husband and was looking for a new home for herself and her two girls, she found a similarly rundown, Spanish-style house with the look to it of a shabby fortress in Westwood Village. She decided to buy it with the money from the sale of her former home. Her father, ostensibly the house expert, begged her not to do it.

"It's a disaster," he told her. "Buying this house will be the biggest mistake of your life."

Convinced of her vision of what it could become, however, she went ahead and bought it and within a year had transformed it into the remarkably lovely house and gardens I had come to know and cherish.

And so it was to be again. She bought this new monster. And after six months of the full-time labor of the two of us and of Riane's cherished housekeeper who came up with us from Los Angeles (whose shyness I had originally mistaken for animosity), plus the labor of carpenters, plumbers, electricians, painters, and gardeners, she worked the same magic all over again.

What emerged out of the process was a unique home in a village renowned for such. Underneath all the grime and neglect the house turned out to be a rare example of the ingenuity of one of the village's most famous original builders, Hugh Comstock. Best-known for his Hansel and Gretel houses and Comstock adobes, he had in two rare instances combined the Mediterranean look of white stucco with the sumptuous wood paneled interior look of an English manor house.

The surrounding gardens, which within another year she had almost restored to their original glory, set off the house like a diamond on velvet. The oaks, which I originally found to be so oppressive and gloomy, now seemed to offer the protective embrace of the most loyal and cheerful of guardians. The wall, which I had felt was an unfriendly presence, now seemed to be just the right height and circumference for asserting a barrier against the outside world.

David Loye

Indeed, the massive beams within the house, the foundation so securely embedded in rock that in over 70 years no earthquake had succeeded in opening any discernible cracks in its stucco walls, and other aspects—including the confusion its sprawl had originally bred in one unfamiliar with it—made of it a home that now seemed just right.

It became the retreat from which we departed for Greece, Italy, Germany, Kenya, and other exotic places in the many lands to which we were to travel—always to return to this home and the embrace of the wall and the oaks and pines and flowers that usually seemed as glad to see us as we were glad to see them again.

This home that, as here, beyond the first 100 poems for Riane, I was to write of many other times.

> The roses in our garden are sturdy
> fellows, stolid, planted deep.
> You would never think they could be
> the least bit visionary and
> then suddenly they are wearing
> these astonishing velvet caps
> like mind's ultimate image of
> who we are and what we could be
> in deepest orange, and pink, and red.
> The gladiolas burst up before me as
> I write—I like these tall, slim
> folk with spray on spray of purple,
> yellow, rose-red and salmon-red
> ascending, ever ascending.
> The marguerites are everywhere,
> their splendid little heads of white
> and yellow clustered together,
>
> (continued)

3,000 Years of Love

nodding to each other, all atwitter
with the gossip of the morning.
In hopeful puffs of blue the lone
bachelor button says, "Here I am,"
and all over the wet earth the
nasturtiums are laughing gaily,
going up, down, around—like orange
dolphins at play in a sea of green.
Walking among them, you are the
presence they've been waiting for.
Their voices still, now the garden
is calm, expectant, all aglow.
To think that such wonder is here!
Proclaim it to the universe, stop
time, somewhere fix it forever!
To see this wonder, how it's mirrored,
you in them and they in you.

NINE
RIANE'S EARLIER LIFE

As she came to write and speak of many times, the turning point in Riane's early life was the Nazi takeover of Austria in 1938.

While Austrians often claim they were invaded by the Germans, in reality most Austrians welcomed the Anschluss or annexation, and the new Nazi government. This, and the continuing Austrian anti-Semitism, made it painful for Riane to travel to her native land.

She had first returned in the 1970s, but even a decade later when I traveled with her to Vienna where she was to give an important talk to a European conference on what could be done to undo the devastation of our global environment, it was still hard for her.

I can still see her as she came from the stage after her talk received a standing ovation. She was sobbing with relief.

"They love me! They love me!" she cried—and I then saw how much, out of the well of fear from a half century earlier, on one level wholly irrational but on another inescapably enduring, she had to fight the fear she'd be mobbed or otherwise rejected.

I could sense the tension in her from the moment we first saw the mighty Gothic grandeur of St.Stephen's Cathedral from the air, and then on landing, and during the drive into the city.

As a little girl she had lived in an apartment along the Danube

3,000 Years of Love

Canal, across the Quai, a center of the old city. Now, as if symbolizing the obliteration of all that once was, a large modern building housing the IBM headquarters stood where her home had been. We walked across the bridge to the Quai and the street of shops on the other side.

"There's where we used to stop for ice cream," she said, her eyes dancing with delight.

"And there's where we bought hot buns! We walked here, my father held my hand, this was our special time together!"

She broke off, tears in her eyes.

She had been born into the home of a relatively well-to-do Jewish couple in Vienna in 1931. Her father was a distributor of fine cutlery—perfectly honed knives of Solingen, exquisite manicure sets from Switzerland. He was handsome, dapper, a charmer. Her mother was an attractive blonde with soulful blue eyes and a shy smile. Their marriage was not ideal, but as an only child, Riane basked in their attention in her early years.

Then, almost literally overnight, everything changed. For months she had felt the strange new fear at work in her parents. Gradually she saw the fear reflected in the tight faces, mutterings, and haunted eyes of other Jews. Abruptly the woman who had taken care of her as far back as she could remember, her beloved Mitzi, left—later she came to know it was not because she herself had been bad, as she feared, but because a new law forbade Gentiles from working in Jewish households.

One day came the jolt of seeing a white-bearded old Jew surrounded by a jeering crowd forcing him to scrub the sidewalk on his knees.

Then came the first glimpse into the horror that became the Holocaust. On November 10, 1938, came the infamous Kristallnacht or "night of broken glass." Organized by the Nazis in from Germany and home grown, mobs roamed Vienna. Citywide the crash could be heard as they smashed the windows of Jewish shops and homes. Throughout the city flames shot up, Jews screamed while others laughed and yelled. Looting, burning, they beat all the Jews they could lay their hands on. 195 synagogues were burned, more than 800 shops destroyed, 7500 looted.

That night the Nazis also began to haul off the Jews to be railroaded to the prison camps where they were first to become slave laborers and later put to death in the gas chambers. Riane's father was one of 20,000 seized that night.

Watching in horror from behind her mother in the doorway, she saw him kicked down the long flight of stairs that ascended to their apartment into the arms of the mob of thugs below. She then saw what transfixed both her and the Nazis watching in astonishment. Her mother began to rage at them.

Who did they think they were? They couldn't do this to her husband. They must give him back, she fearlessly insisted.

Had it been the fact she was blue-eyed and blonde and didn't look Jewish? Did they think they might have made a mistake? Had it been they were taught to fear authority? That here must be a woman with some power if she dared to stand up to and speak to them in this way?

For whatever reason, the Gestapo officer in charge told Riane's mother he would see about giving her husband back if she brought a large sum of money to Gestapo headquarters. This she did, they hid her father in the attic, and as soon as they were able to, they fled Vienna, leaving everything behind.

There were at that time only two relatively open ports to which the

Jews of Europe might flee. Over the entire face of this earth, there were only the two—Havana, Cuba, or Shanghai, in China.

Being considered important enough, England admitted Sigmund Freud when he fled Austria in the same year, 1938. But Riane and her parents and all the "ordinary" Jews could only find refuge in Havana or Shanghai. Even Great Britain, after a history of being the great bastion of freedom and refuge for the persecuted of all nations historically, was cocked against them. Not only did the British promote formation of the Arab League and arm the Arabs against the Jews in Palestine. Even after Germany was defeated and the war ended, British ships patrolled the seas to keep boatloads of Jewish concentration camp survivors from landing in Palestine, where the beachhead that became the state of Israel in 1948 was finally established.

Think of this. How would you feel if you were a Jew and discovered there were only two places on the face of all this wide earth you could flee to? Only two places where a fierce hatred or a massive indifference didn't prevail. Only two places where still not a crumb of love was to be found, but at least for a while one might find an uncertain toleration. Havana in one far off, Spanish speaking spot of land? Or Shanghai, to struggle with wholly alien customs and unknowns and the mystery of the Chinese language at the other end of the earth?

And then, in response to bribes and pressure from the Nazis, Havana was denied them.

For Riane and her parents were on one of the last ships allowed to dock. They had been in Havana barely a year when the St.Louis with over 900 Jewish refugees was turned back.

As Riane writes of the St.Louis in her novel *Dreamwalking in Havana,* the ship stood there in the bay for weeks while Jewish agencies in the U.S. frantically tried to raise enough ransom money to satisfy the Cuban government and allow them to land. But so great was the pressure and the prejudice that their landing was still denied.

Cruising north, the St.Louis and Jewish agencies in the United States desperately sought permission for the ship to land in Miami or any other U.S. port—but were again denied. Closely watched and apparently orchestrated by the Nazis, this evidence of the world's indifference to the plight of the Jews became another green light to proceed with building the death camps and the gas chambers.

Unlike the six million other Jews caught behind in Europe, to be murdered by the Nazis, Riane and her parents had been able to make it to Cuba, but they had lost almost everything they owned. Now there was nothing to live on but a small allowances from the Jewish agency. The contrast with the elegance and security of life in Vienna before the Nazis could not have been more drastic. Now they lived in rank-smelling old boarding houses, with the fear and unhappiness of other Jews now forced to scratch for a living, the indifference or antagonism of slum-dwelling Cubans, and large cockroaches as their fellow tenants.

Riane tells of how in one boarding house one night she had to go to the bathroom and her father took her down to the single bathroom for all at the end of the hall.

They entered to wonder why the walls and ceiling were painted black. Her father pulled the chain to turn on the single light bulb overhead—and the black walls dissolved into hundreds of huge cockroaches who descended on them in a filthy cloud. They screamed and ran—she remembers what a shock it was to see her father trembling for so long afterward, head in his hands.

Prohibited by law from gainful employment on the ground this would take jobs from Cuban workers, deciding that somehow he had to get them out of the misery of this boarding house life, her father noticed the Cubans were everywhere selling crude tourist items made of alligator skin. Remembering the fine crocodile purses and other goods in Vienna and Paris, he decided to establish a fine alligator goods business in Havana. Soon, he became, in effect, the Alligator King of Cuba.

Behind the alligators lay another part of the story destined to drive her later work. The factory was in the Havana industrial slums. They lived in an apartment on top of a tenement with a high up bridge to span the alley and connect to the alligator factory.

As she writes of in her first novel *Dreamwalking in Havana,* a gate that could be locked on the long flight of stairs down to the street came to symbolize both protection from the world and all that barred the way to a better world. Growing up here among the poorest of Cubans, with Havana's red light district nearby, daily she unlocked the gate to descend to the street to walk to the street car that took her to the trees and flowers and the private school to which the children of the wealthiest of Cubans were sent.

Daily shuffling between the grimy world of poverty and the beauty and bounty of the world of wealth, the contrast provided a new level of culture shock to embed an enduring message. Now atop the injustice of the global persecution of Jews, she was the sensitive child exposed to the global injustice of the wide disparity between rich and poor. And to complete the picture there was the slum's favorite sport for the Cuban men—feeling women's and even little girls' bottoms and fronts and snickering and joking.

Along with all the other assaults of machismo that saturated layers and aspects of Cuban society, this became the vivid grounding in Riane's memory for the perception of vast injustice of the subjugation of women by men that later became a core drive for her work.

When she was fourteen, Riane and her parents finally gained entry to the U.S. Finding the weather, the opportunities, and the reassurance of the Jewish community in Los Angeles congenial, for a time her life settled down to "normal."

By now she was an immigrant who not only spoke fluent Spanish, but also German and English with an impressive upper-class British accent. She excelled in high school. She went on to excel at UCLA and UC-Berkeley, focusing primarily on sociology and anthropology, graduating summa cum laude. She started law school at UCLA, but then quit when she married the following summer. It was the 1950s, and after the "Rosie the Rivetter" years of World War II, women were being pressured to return to their domestic roles.

From the start, Riane's was not a happy marriage. Like thousands of other women at the time, she was discovering that marriage could be a straitjacket rather than a liberation. She had married a man she barely knew. The more they got to know each other, the less they got along and the more unhappy the marriage became. Still, people did not get divorced in those days. Marriage was supposed to be for life, for better or worse, and the pressure from Riane's parents against divorce was especially powerful.

She left a couple of times, but was pressured to return by her mother. She tried to make the best of it. Using some of the money her parents had given them as a wedding present, she and her husband went to Europe and then for a time lived in Israel.

It was just after the new nation had reasserted its right to life through victory against what became a series of wars launched by Egypt, Syria,

Lebanon, Iraq, and Jordan. First hand, she knew how it was to run the gauntlet of roads under Palestinian sniper fire, to hear the deadly drum of the call on the radio to shove the Jews back into the sea. Her husband, one of the early computer engineers, got a job at the Weizmann Institute to help lay the ground for this industry, which later proved decisive in Israel's economic growth and defense.

When they returned to the U.S., she tried a number of jobs—seemingly random at the time, but further storing up and cumulating real world rather than just book experience to shape and figure in her later books, theories, and social action.

Foreshadowing her later development as a theorist and macro-historian, she worked as a systems scientist for the Systems Development Corporation. An offshoot of the Rand Corporation, at the time SDC was a West Coast "think tank" for the U.S. military-industrial-complex. It was also a hotbed for the new field of futures studies then being shaped by Herman Kahn, in which Riane's work later figured. For a time she worked as a construction supervisor in her parent's building business. But the impact of her home life on herself and her two daughters was becoming intolerable. Like thousands of other women at the time, she decided she had to find a way of breaking free. She went back to and finished UCLA law school and got a part time job with a Beverly Hills entertainment law firm.

Then came a pivotal turning point.

"Within a period of three months I quit my job, my marriage, and smoking," she says of the time. She also became involved in heady, early, formative years for the rise of the counterculture of the civil rights, economic justice, anti-war, and women's movements.

This was in the sixties, that time of breaking loose in all the directions out of which the women's movement was getting underway on the West Coast. She switched from entertainment to family law to fight for the rights of women and children in divorce cases. She became involved in the legal side of the women's political struggle, writing and campaigning in Sacramento for the passage of laws by the California legislature advancing the rights of women and children. She was a co-founder of the Los Angeles Women's Center, one of the first in the nation. She also founded the first center on women and the law in the United States, the L.A. Women's Legal Center, and taught pioneering courses in women's history and law at Immaculate Heart College and UCLA, which led to formation of a women's studies department at UCLA.

It was an amazing performance, for the first time revealing the enormous store of passion and energy her past of all too few places and, despite the awful yearning, such low expectations for love had imprisoned within her. Now released by the 1960s women's liberation movement, apparently rising out of her like a tornado, came the drive spurred by her memories of Nazi Austria, Cuba, and her extended family of grandparents, uncles, aunts, cousins throughout Europe—whom she had prayed for throughout the war, who with the war's end she came to know had almost all perished in the gas chambers.

On and on the energy and the passion surged. Out of her knowledge of constitutional law, in which she had excelled at the UCLA Law School, she wrote an amicus curiae, or "friend of the court" brief for a law suit before the U.S. Supreme Court, arguing that women should be considered "persons" under the Equal Protection clause of the 14th Amendment. This helped pave the way for the historic Reed v. Reed decision, which for the first time struck down a law blatantly discriminating on the basis of sex.

For a client couple she wrote the original prenuptial document that became the model for a new marriage contract. The idea was to get men and women to sign a legally-binding marriage contract that would protect women's rights, which the laws of the time did not. This was not only to prevent all the pain, acrimony, and expense of adversarial divorces, but to lay the ground for equality during the marriage. She was invited to Sweden to lecture on this innovation. The British equivalent of *Life* magazine in the U.S. gave major coverage to her and her story. Later, also based on her legal work, she wrote *Dissolution: No-Fault Divorce, Marriage, and the Future of Women*.

Published by McGraw-Hill shortly before we met, this book accurately predicted the feminization of poverty that later came to prevail in America.

Throughout it all—marching in protests, boycotting, lecturing widely, fund-raising, helping to stage events—she became a well-known leader in the West Coast women's movement, thereby a pioneer in the great surge during the second half of the 20th century that at last put gender equality significantly on the map politically, economically, and socially in the United States and globally.

But while on one hand she was growing and expanding publicly, finding an exciting and meaningful place in the thrust of the massed force of progressive movements that drive human evolution ahead, in the private life that equally factors in human evolution she was physically and psychologically being torn apart.

By the time of the birth of her second child—she did not want her daughter to be a lonely only child, as she had been—she had become so unhappy in her marriage that she began to think of suicide. Only concern for her two little daughters kept her from going ahead with it.

But here again was another twist to the screw of the widening situation for the new freedom of ambition and aspiration for the "new woman" of the time. Despite her love for her children, she was unable to give them the care, even the emotional presence, they needed. She was too absorbed in her own misery, congealed by pain. Because of the dislocations of her own early life and the lack of good parenting instruction materials available in those years, she also did not have the skills for good parenting. Nor did she have a partner to parent with, as her husband, who had also had a very difficult childhood, lacked what was needed.

Ahead lay all the decades I have now watched as Riane worked to try to make up for the past and build a close, open relationship with her daughters. Wounds still remain. A great and persisting sorrow in Riane's life is the pain her failings, followed by her own physical and emotional collapse, caused her children. But one of her great joys has been to see her daughters become extraordinarily fine mothers to her grandchildren in all the ways she wishes she had been herself.

And so it was for Riane a time of liberation but also of enormous stress, as trying to juggle her family, her work as an attorney, and her growing involvement in social causes took its toll. There were the problems and the devastating let downs of the love life of the single mother. There was, in Riane's case, the additionally agonizing pressure of having to contend with the uncomprehending and at times aghast censure of her divorce by the parents to whom she was so closely bonded by the time of being hunted and the years thereafter of survival.

With first the unexpected death of her father and shortly thereafter the sudden death of her mother, whom she found dead when she went to her house, came a revival of the terrors of Riane's early years in Austria and Cuba. Coupled with all her other accumulated stresses, this now took a physical form, afflicting her body with one ailment after another. Finally, she collapsed.

It was no temporary in-and-out sort of thing. It was near total collapse, physically and emotionally, with only the fierce drive of her mind remaining, and this too was endangered. It was a few years afterward that I came into her life.

TEN
MY EARLY LIFE

As for Riane, the big question in my early life was also the tantalizing, and in my case ultimately the numbing and quite literally dumbing down, uncertainty of love, and the existence of evil.

The strongest memories I have of my early years are of my first encounters with what eventually, with no quibbling or qualifying, I came to see was indeed evil, and with its opposite: the existence of good.

I go back in seeing and feeling, and find myself, age five or so, in my first day at school. For some time I had been eagerly anticipating this next step up, this first venturing out into the wider world in a new and highly touted special way. I had apparently been shown the school and the route to it beforehand so that the baffling and uncertain person who was my mother must have felt confident I could make it safely by myself that first day.

It was a proud moment, an exciting moment. As I approached the school a small boy who seemed to be about half my size came running toward me.

"My first friend," I thought with delight.

An instant later this little total stranger punched me in the stomach with a force of such wholly senseless ferocity that I see now further shattered what there was of fragile and tenuous stability in my world into

3,000 Years of Love

an abiding distrust.

Hardly the jack boot march of the Nazis into one's life. More like the surreal cruelty that was the stock in trade for conversion into so-called humor by the worst of Charlie Chaplin, the Three Stooges, or the cartoons. But all the childhood cruelties of bullies and snobs, of the existence of all the little thieves, liars, and cheaters who got away with it, along with the devastation of a more prolonged and complicated day and night of horror too involved to go into here, cumulated into my sense of the force at work in a generally loveless world that I came to know was rightfully called evil.

In sharp contrast was what I knew of the unshakeable, and I felt then and still feel eternal love of the two great pillars of my early life. These were my grandmother on my father's side and my grandfather on my mother's side.

My own parents were, by comparison, uncertain mysteries, my father nice but remote, my mother demanding and cold. But Grandmother Loye seemed to me the collection of all that was reliably good in the world.

A matter of fact Northern Baptist, she was an extremely bright, highly organized, and artistically gifted woman who put what in our time would have gone into some remarkable career into the job of mother, homemaker, and good works volunteer. She was a continual fountain of instruction as to what was right and what was wrong. I adored her and she adored me. In her presence I always felt aglow.

On the wall of our dining room today are two of her paintings along with another painting by my daughter Kathryn. They tell much of the change across three generations. Kathryn's a bold and liberated abstract splash of ascending gradations of reds melding into purples. My grandmother's conventional still lifes of the time—in one case of three apples, in the other of a small graceful jug and an onion—but executed with love and care and precision, and conveying the essential greatness of character that was unquestionably hers.

A completely different sort of person was my grandfather C.W.Sanders, of whom I've written at length in *Brave Laughter*. Manager of one of the best known book stores in the country, early encourager of Sinclair Lewis and F.Scott Fitzgerald, known throughout the trade as one of the great book sellers of his time, he sat me on his lap and used to enchant me with hair-raising, crime-busting tales he made up supposedly about the St.Paul police force. Predating Superman, his and my hero was a "Captain Duffy" who used to reduce the thugs to jelly with his standard threat to cease and desist or he would "cut your nick off!"

A tale of course sure to give the willies to child psychologists today. But I see now how beyond this from him I gained my sense of the male virtue of a caring transcending the stereotypes of gender. A mountain of a man physically, gifted athlete as well as book worm—witty, playful, every bit a "man's man," who each week played poker and pool with "the boys"—he also served as the household shopper and the nurturant and loving mother as well as father to his seven children. His father before him and his brother were the same. Strong, funny, loving, nurturant and playful—the children came to them with their problems.

In contrast to my grandmother Loye, he was a fervent atheist who in his will insisted he not be given a Christian burial. But like her, he too was not only firm on what was right and what was wrong, but, with a roaring capacity for the raging language and the thunderbolt aura of a Jehovah, he would freely raise hell if aroused by any cause.

3,000 Years of Love

Had fate given me these two pillars to live with, my life would have been entirely different. But instead our contact was too brief and then they were dead and I was psychically left alone to fend for myself in what seemed to me well into middle age—as well as often still today—an alien world.

Six years before Riane was born in Vienna, my own life had begun almost halfway around the earth, in the basking warmth and the palm trees of Palo Alto, California, where my father was a graduate student at Stanford. When I was a year old, we moved back to the sub-zero dead-of-winter shock of Minnesota, home for both my mother's and father's families. Here my two sisters were born and with the upheaval of the first historical event to impact on us, the Great Depression of the early 1930s, my family moved to Oklahoma.

My father had been out of work for two years when out of the bleak succession of days going nowhere a school chum from his Stanford years called with an offer of a job in the oil industry. Thus while Hitler was gaining power in Europe, I was a child growing up in a raw land then littered with mile after mile of oil derricks pumping around the clock to drain the earth of this "black gold" from what less than a century earlier had been Indian land.

When the Whites expanded into the West, Oklahoma Territory became, quite literally, the dumping ground for all the tribes shoved from their original lands. For most of them this meant the degraded and impoverished life that was the standard for forcibly displaced Indians then as well as all too often still now. A tiny minority of the Indians, however, chiefly around where I lived, had by their standards become enormously wealthy because of the discovery of oil under Osage land. For many years, I too still drew a tiny bit of royalty yearly from those

Osage lands.

This disparity between rich and poor among the Indians was writ large in a way I could never forget in the situation of the Whites in the town where I grew up. Its name, Bartlesville, suggests a hick town off in the middle of nowhere. But during the 1930s it had the second highest wealth per capita in the United States. It was the world headquarters for three major oil companies. In microcosm it reflected all that later came to most disturb me about my country, America, and its relationship to the rest of this planet, and to all the peoples of this earth.

At one extreme Bartlesville was this tiny world of enormous wealth, of baronial estates, of lavish parties, of the elegant golf course and country club to which my family belonged. Over the entire block next to where I lived on Cherokee avenue sprawled the palatial home of the founder of the premier oil company, Phillips Petroleum. But quite literally across the tracks, as in most American cities then, lived the underclass invisible except at Christmas, when it was popular to ask for "nuts and candy for the poor children" in one's letters to Santa.

Here the Mexicans, Blacks, Indians who preferred to live in town off the reservation, and poor Whites lived in shacks on the land that nobody else wanted. Despoiled by pollution from "The Smelters"— the huge zinc smeltering plant that provided the area's chief source of employment in manufacturing, and from oil wells pumped dry and then abandoned—the soil beneath and around the shacks was, by turns, slick with oil, or crusted by a white deposit, such that even weeds found it hard to grow.

From growing up in that town—and later working in the oil fields, covering Big Oil as a newsman, and as claimant in one of the thousands of lawsuits by people routinely robbed of royalties by oil companies with hordes of lawyers to keep the cases tied down forever in court—I came to know something that has roared back into life again with vengeance as I finish this book.

Over half a century before it tried to seize the 21st century, I came to know the essentially lawless and self-seeking Bush, Cheney, Rove, Rumsfeld mentality that in an incredible legalized coup d'etat came to power in America—and to hate it with a passion.

Although my father, and the fathers of almost all my friends, were staunchly and even fiercely Republican, for reasons I still do not fully understand, I grew up even more fiercely committed to Roosevelt, the New Deal, and the Democrats.

This I believed with a conviction I could then feel, but not yet adequately express, was the only avenue I knew of that seemed to offer any hope for changing the situation of the people "across the tracks." But gradually I also became aware of an even larger concern.

My father became president of the local Chamber of Commerce. He also became, over time I came to see, both aghast and fascinated, the town's chief fascist. As head of the Bartlesville chapter of the America First Committee, he preached the doctrine there was nothing to fear from Hitler, and even if there was, it was best to leave "them" to fight it out without "us" getting involved again in "their" squabbles. But in the sharpest possible contrast, I look back now and see myself and in that whole town one other boy I knew for who we were and our significance at that place and in that time. Driven I see now by a higher intelligence and the immeasurably wider sensitivity that is the great hope out of every new generation for evolution, we two and once in a while other sons of those blinded fathers were resonating to the voices on the radio of Roosevelt and Churchill, as well as H.V. Kaltenborn and Edward R.

Murrow and the other great news commentators of that day, and to what was happening of concern and horror in the world beyond Bartlesville.

There I was in high school in this self-centered and self-contained little Oklahoma town of enormous wealth, while in Europe, ostensibly unknown to me as well as to most other Americans at the time, the Nazis were hauling the Jews off to the death camps and thousands such as Riane and her parents were fleeing for their lives. Yet looking back on those days, I am struck by how in that town of an overwhelming isolationist indifference it was almost as though I was already, by some psychic connection, picking up what was happening to Riane, and her parents, and the 6,000,000 who never escaped.

Thereafter my life sort of flopped in place and zig-zagged with an always absorbing but essentially crazy-quilt pattern into early middle age. Still in high school, during summers I was a factory worker, a farm hand, and a "shooter's helper" handling dynamite and facing oblivion on a seismograph crew in the oil fields. World War II came. Filled with visions of fighting the horror of Hitler, I enlisted in the Navy. But instead of going on to fight, and quite possibly die, and gain the romantic watery grave that was the Navy's consolation, I was shunted into a mild version of the surreal side to war that Joseph Heller wrote of in his cock-eyed novel *Catch 22*.

Tested and labeled too smart for cannon fodder, I was first sent to college for officer training, then busted and ultimately sent to join a secret propaganda war corps formed by the U.S. Navy to fight the U.S. Army and the U.S. Air Force under the leadership of Carolyn Keene, author of the Nancy Drew mystery stores. No, I am not making this up. Some day I will write it up. In the end I finally got to actually board a ship and go to sea as a very young Navy news correspondent. Working out of secret headquarters in Washington I at last knew the incredible sense of adventure unique to the storms and the calm of a ship on the high seas that years later, to my delight I discovered, had down the coast of South America traced the same route and docked in the same ports as had the young Charles Darwin on the famous voyage of the Beagle over 100 years earlier.

All too short. But ah, what a time!

After the War I worked as a bellhop and as a room service waiter to support myself while completing college at Dartmouth. After graduating with a B.S. in 1948, to support a wife and soon four children back in Oklahoma, I became a radio station program director, a film producer, a magazine editor, and a television newsmen back in the brand new medium's great Ed Murrow early days. Moving at what seemed to me then the advanced age of thirty-five to Princeton, New Jersey, I worked in Manhattan for the world's largest and at the time probably most evil public relations agency, then as an account exec for a Madison Avenue advertising agency.

Looking back I can see now how every bit of this scattered and seemingly senseless wandering proved invaluable in providing me with such a wide range of experience within the working realities of mid-century America. At the time, however, there ground at me the horrifying sense that I had originally set out to go somewhere of importance, but had somehow wholly lost my way, and now most horribly and surely would never get there.

From the recurring pattern for the nightmares I still find impossible to shake once asleep I see now how deeply the frustration and this fear was stamped into me back in those years. Other than the love I had for my first wife and for our children in the main track for my life at that time, what held me together was the conviction in the other, often secret track that kept me obsessively writing, writing, writing on the side.

No matter how repellent, boring, or painful I found any part of my early life what kept me going was that I could tell myself it was just grist for the mill of The Great American Novel I was writing. But after grinding out three of them that failed to gain publication, I found myself facing the early "mid-life crisis" that roars in to seize and shake all of us who have aspired to and failed to attain our early dreams.

I was forced to see that in the direction I had been going lay not the morally better world that my grandmother believed in and worked for, or that my grandfather raged about, and laid about right and left with gusto to insist on, but only another ground under nobody at the end of the line. I saw I was nearing forty with no longer any meaningful creative identity. I saw that without some kind of radical change I would be just one more blinded and faceless slave serving the world as it is rather than the world as it could and *should* be.

The choice, I decided, was between prolonged psychoanalysis to rebuild myself and hopefully find purpose in life, or go back to school to start over again.

I chose school because it seemed that in this direction I could at least come out with a more meaningful job at the end. Soon I abruptly switched from journalism, public relations, and advertising to a job as a "senior writer" for the big factory for the SAT, Educational Testing Service in Princeton. ETS at the time put the money from its tests into one of the world's largest and most advanced research centers for education. Working there and feeding in and out of it were some of the world's leading psychologists. It was a truly heavenly arrangement, as my job was to write about them and their research while working on my own doctorate.

After a day's work at the big test factory for a decade I slogged an hour into Manhattan to night school at the old New School for Social Research, now New School University, in Greenwich Village, then nightly another hour back to Princeton.

I excelled in all courses, shot through all other hurdles, gained the admiration and friendship of some of the great psychologists of that day. But in another replay of the story I came to hear from others up against the prejudice of the traditional academic against the independent minded late bloomer with a nontraditional background and large ambitions of a disruptive originality, it took the rejection of 18 full dissertation proposals, the years of research for two completed dissertations also rejected, and, at last, the chance intervention of a famous psychologist disgusted with the injustice of the treatment I was receiving, before a third dissertation was finally accepted, and I graduated in 1972 with my doctorate in social psychology.

Out of those years of a relentless drive to find myself and a meaningful future my first marriage was shattered and my children left with an abiding sense of neglect. But out of those years came the first triumph, the first recognition, the first signal pointing the way toward the role in helping to build the better world I sought.

On top of everything else I had managed to write *The Healing of a Nation*. Earlier, despite the enthusiastic endorsements of leading authorities in its subject area, when I had submitted the manuscript of this book for my dissertation it had been rejected by the chief academic sadist who year after year had blocked me. But now I had the satisfaction of seeing this book, my first, a psychohistory, go on to win a top national award earlier given to Martin Luther King and to the great

Swedish economist Gunnar Myrdal for his classic *An American Dilemma.*

Which in turn led to my being invited to join the faculty of the Princeton University psychology department.

Which in turn opened up the way for the out-of-the-blue hiring that took me to California and the UCLA School of Medicine to head a pioneering research project.

Which in turn put me in the right place at the right time to meet Riane—and to thumb my nose at everything and everybody who over the long prior years had, as if a Satanic curse had been laid on me by an adverse fate, belittled or blocked my getting to where I wanted to go.

ELEVEN
ITALY, UNCLE MAIER, AND THE
GLACIER AND THE FLAME

When I think back on our life together, much comes to mind. Riane, day in and day out, reading, writing, working on book after book. With her daughters and her grandchildren, playing and laughing, teaching her granddaughter chess or her grandsons croquet. Strolling through our garden, picking flowers for those extraordinary bouquets she places throughout the house. The two of us walking together on the palisades overlooking Carmel beach, so often ecstatic with the sight of the sunset, the flight of pelicans across the sky, the roll and white explosion of the waves ceaselessly driven to touch, and again and again and again touch the shore.

Often now, bound by infirmities and the feeling one has surely by now seen enough of the world, and has come more to treasure the journeys of the mind, I think of our trips—the wonder of all those new places, and getting to know all the wonderful people and causes we came to know and care about.

For Riane, one of the most beloved of these people was her Uncle Maier, her mother's younger brother. After the death of both her parents, he was the only survivor of the life she had lost through the Nazi terror. Our first meeting with Maier was in 1984. Riane and I flew to Rome and he flew there from Dusseldorf so we could meet in the place he loved and had lived and worked in prior to the Holocaust.

I remember landing at the airport, the long taxi in through the hum drum outer suburbs, and then the entry into wonderland.

Until then, Rome had existed in my mind mainly in drab black and white pictures of some wholly uninteresting ruins in my old high school Latin text book back in Bartlesville in the late 1930s. But here, in reality, the glory of those worn and eloquent stones piled and shaped or strewn among the dark fingers of the cypress trees was overwhelming.

Later on, I became leery of the rocket speed that was normal for Italian cab drivers. But this speed seemed perfection as we shot through the entry into the old and new city through the majestic remnant of the Great Aurelian Wall. And then on the long wide swoop of the thoroughfare that for a time took one, as I recall, past the Palatine Hill, the Capitoline Hill, and Trajan's Forum. It was like the acceleration of a dream, or the movement made possible in movies by fast trucking or a zoom lens. Zam. Zam. Zam, the sights went by as we clasped hands in excitement.

For whatever time there was thereafter, one day, two, three, who can remember, we were like children again drinking it all in. The grand vista looking down into the Piazza di Spagna and the Bernini fountain from the top of the Spanish Steps. The immense precision cut of the Romanic lettering along the face of the Pantheon outside, and then the somber amazement of the dome looking up from inside. The lush grandeur of the church of Santa Maria degli Angeli, which by accident I discovered Michelangelo had hidden inside the ruins of the Baths of Diocletian.

And the walls of the Colosseum, pock marked from what I thought at first must have been an unaccountable firing of cannon balls. But instead I was told these were the thousands of holes left behind when marauding armies pulled off the astonishment of the old walls' ornamental statuary for souvenirs. And of course the lonely grandeur of the Foro Romano, where one could best see what once had been laid out there in buildings and statues of white marble, and lush green gardens—the heart of earth's most mighty city, now the realm of thousands of tourists, mice, and stray cats.

But that of course is only half the charm of Rome. The greater wonder is how the grandeur of the ruins serves as the mighty stage for the vibrant life of the present day. Walking and walking the streets in the evening, we marveled at the sheer joy in living that so often seems the essence of Italy at its best—the restless, peering stream of life that ebbs and flows through all the narrow modern streets up and down which all the people move, lookers, shoppers, buyers bearing their various new treasures, the elegant and the lowly at one.

And here we were and could share this!

However absorbing or moving or breathtaking a sight we came on, this was the feeling we most often remarked on to each other—that we had met seemingly so late in life, but could now go on and on sharing adventures such as this.

And indeed at the time, defying logic but who cares, it did seem as though this could be forever.

She could enjoy the fact this was all new to me, never having visited Europe before. She, having known Rome before, could see it fresh through my eyes. I could revel in the fact she could answer my questions, and spoke Italian, and simply the pleasure of being there in Rome with such an elegant and beautiful woman beside me.

It was as though by magic I had been transported from the Lyric theater in the Oklahoma of my boyhood into the movie I had been watching back then. But now I was the grown hero beside the heroine, escaped at last from an obscure childhood into where I belonged.

Besides our first long and most meaningful time there, we were to know Rome, a day or two at a time, many times thereafter en route to or coming back from the other places in Italy to which mainly two things called us. One was the speaking engagements that pulled Riane to her home continent as her book *The Chalice and the Blade* became in effect an international best-seller. The Finnish edition in 1988. German and French in 1989. Spanish, Portuguese, and British in 1990. Greek in 1992. Russian in 1993. Norwegian and Danish in 1994. Czech in 1995. Italian in 1996. Dutch in 1997. And in 2002 the Israeli edition in Hebrew that read backward, from back to front, with a luscious nude in a wine glass on the cover.

And of course the Japanese edition in 1991, Chinese in 1993, Ukranian in 2002, Korean in 2005, and a third edition in German and a Swedish edition also in 2005, and an Arabic edition and a Brazilian edition in 2006.

In the case of her speaking engagements air travel for me was generally wangled in as part of the bargaining for her honoraria or speaking fee. The other drawing card that provided the invitation and financing to draw us to Europe was my contribution—our involvement with the multinational General Evolution Research Group, or GERG for short, to which I will come.

Aside from its architectural and cultural splendors, the highlight for both of us on that first trip to Rome was Uncle Maier, whom Riane had yearned for years to see again. It was to Maier in Rome she and her parents had first gone in fleeing their home in Austria and the Nazis .

Now we were to stay with him in his old apartment on the hills overlooking the city.

Maier was a genial, gentle, courtly man with greying blonde hair. I could see he had been quite handsome when younger. I quickly came to see he was also, as Riane had said, a man of high intelligence, great sensitivity, with a gentle, playful wit. I liked him immediately. I could see he felt the same toward me. He could speak no English and I no German or Italian, but communicating through gestures and meaningful looks, over the years before he died we became intuitively very close.

We had a little routine that brings a considerable twinge of sadness every time I think of it. Making use of the Americanisms he came to relish, on parting at any point for a few minutes, hours, or a few years, I would say, "See you later, alligator." To which, eyes popping, beaming with delight, he would chortle the stock response, "In a while, crocodile."

It was a great part of our pleasure to see how meaningful to Uncle Maier was this visit by his beloved niece and how great was his pleasure in being able to take us to show us his favorite spots all over Rome. It was also more than a little touching. Here it was he had lived and had his practice as a doctor in the good years, the best years, prior to the horror of the concentration camps. Now, of all places, he was forced to live in Germany, in notably anti-Semitic Dusseldorf in order to be close to his one daughter and his two grandchildren. But renting out the beloved old apartment now and then to cover the expense, to connect with the old life, he had hung onto it in Rome.

His story I was to learn superficially at first. When Riane's parents had arrived with their child, having fled Nazi Austria, Maier had urged them, "Stay with us. You will be safe here. The Italians would never let anything like this happen here."

But from what they had personally experienced of the Nazi horror, Riane's parents were convinced the whole of Europe was doomed. They fled with their child on to Cuba—but for Maier lay ahead the inconceivable. Along with thousands of other Italian Jews, Maier, his wife Bertha and their little girl were seized and shipped off to a concentration camp.

Later I was to learn the rest in detail. Maier had come to visit us in Carmel. He and I were walking in the canyon nearby our home. We were as usual communicating in short bursts of language unintelligible to the other except by intuition when suddenly he became very agitated, so much so my first impulse was the fear of a heart attack. But somehow I guessed something had triggered the memory and he was struggling to speak of the concentration camp years.

Perhaps it was because he felt secure here, an ocean and a continent away from the horror and among people in Riane and me whom he felt were safe and could understand. I sensed the moment had come when driven by the need for catharsis he must unload or explode.

I rushed him home, alerted Riane, set up the tape recorder, and for the next three days Maier mainly sat at our dining room table unloading everything in German to Riane.

It was the tale not only of the horror of life in concentration camp after concentration camp, and of seeing their only child, their beautiful little daughter, die. One of the most devastating parts of his account was how he had survived while everybody else had been killed.

The standard scenario was of the announcement over the camp loud speaker that everybody was to prepare to move on to another camp. The day or night before the move he would be pulled aside by the German camp commander. Again and again he was told that, as the others streamed out of the camp, a certain door in a certain building they were passing would open. He was to step through that door and let the rest go on.

He came to hope the case was otherwise, but later came to know the rest had gone on to the gas chambers. As for himself, he was saved ostensibly because he was a doctor and the Nazis wanted to keep him as a practical matter. Doctors could be useful. But from hearing the tale from Riane, I came to see the deeper and larger story. Being blonde and Aryan handsome, Maier did not "look Jewish." He was also a man of great charm and obvious simple goodness.

I saw that in his case, beyond the excuse of his being a doctor, he had apparently become the token Jew spared to salve whatever remained of conscience in these men whose job it was to be monsters.

When he became sure of what was going on, all he wanted to do was die with the rest. But there was his wife Bertha to care for. Each time he refused to stay behind unless Bertha was also spared. So all during the war years prior to liberation he was forced to live on and on in the concentration camps knowing that everyone else—all those who in drove after drove he came to know and care for both as a doctor and as a human being—were marked for the death chamber.

For those of us who lived then, one of the difficulties has been in finding words, metaphors, or images sufficiently powerful to convey even a fraction of the enormity of the Nazis. In the tour de force of *The Chalice and the Blade*, Riane was to powerfully define what spawned them as the Domination way of life, which over 5,000 years replaced the earlier Partnership way of life as the ruling model for our species.

For me the image became that of the chill immensity of the Glacier that continually rolls down into our lives to try to snuff out the Flame of freedom and equality.

TWELVE
RIANE'S BOOKS

"Why do we hunt and persecute each other? Why is our world so full of man's infamous inhumanity to man—and to woman? How can human beings be so brutal to their own kind? What is it that chronically tilts us toward cruelty rather than kindness, toward war rather than peace, toward destruction rather than actualization?"

Going straight as an arrow to the target of all our bloody centuries, these are the simple yet searing questions Riane raises in opening *The Chalice and the Blade*.

"Of all life-forms on this planet," she continues, "only we can plant and harvest fields, compose poetry and music, seek truth and justice, teach a child to read and write-or even laugh and cry. Because of our unique ability to imagine new realities and realize these through ever more advanced technologies, we are quite literally partners in our own evolution. And yet, this same wondrous species of ours now seems bent on putting an end not only to its own evolution but to that of most life on our globe, threatening our planet with ecological catastrophe or nuclear annihilation."

"The search for answers to these questions led me to the re-examination of our past, present, and future on which this book is based."

Part of the difference Riane brought to her books and theories was that she used a different method of inquiry. She drew from a much larger data base than other studies—one that, as she writes, takes into account the *whole* of human history (including our prehistory), the *whole* of humanity (both its female and male halves), and the *whole* of our lives (both the public and the private sphere of family and other intimate relations). To do this, she was uniquely prepared not only by her systems background but by her new consciousness of how the situation, needs, contributions, and aspirations of no less than half of humanity – women – were not considered important enough to be included in most earlier studies, which were quite aptly called "the study of man."

But there was more. I see her work as representing a special merging of two historic streams. One was the stream of the gene pool of the Jewish past, shaped by the injustice of an immense suffering but also by an unusual capacity for joy. Out of this melding so hauntingly captured by all forms of Jewish music and much of Jewish humor, she was born with an extremely high intelligence, a great innate sensitivity, and the high energy potential one almost always finds driving unusual accomplishment.

The other stream was the impact of the circumstances of her early life—the Nazi experience, the pros and cons of being a woman at this point in human evolution, the window these impacts provide into what became her challenge to the Domination way of life and her vision of the Partnership way.

The first phase of her published writing emerged out of her training as a lawyer, her resonation to the plight of woman, and her determination to become a champion of the rights of women and children. *Dissolution:*

3,000 Years of Love

No-Fault Divorce, Marriage, and the Future of Women, published by McGraw-Hill in 1977, tackled the problems the subtitle indicates head on. No-fault divorce was then a new idea offering both women and men an appealing chance to divorce without having to hassle over who was to blame for what. The down side she pointed out, however, was that it was going to allow men to leave many penniless women in their wake. Because of this and similar prospects, in the book she predicted the "feminization of poverty" that later became a grievous social fact.

Dissolution was published shortly after we met. Then—with my aid as a researcher, writer, and when no one else would touch it, by default a literary agent—she wrote the definitive mass paperback in the fight for passage of the Equal Rights Amendment (ERA) to the U.S. Constitution, *The Equal Rights Handbook*.

The book was a "quickie" turned out to provide the women's movement and other activist groups with a handbook for the fight for passage of the proposed Equal Rights Amendment to the U.S. Constitution. Published as a mass paperback by Avon in 1978, it was rushed into circulation to try to get the word out on how best to advance the cause against the massive campaign to stop it launched by political and religious rightwingers.

All that was proposed by the ERA was this single line for the whole Amendment: "Equality of rights shall not be denied or abridged by the United States or any state on the basis of sex." Yet in the first eruption of what became the successful alternation of stealth and holy war soon to swallow whole the Republican party and inexorably drive toward the disaster of the Bush years, the rightist-fundamentalist alliance defeated it by successfully selling the idea it would destroy the family and actually hurt rather than help women.

David Loye

It was this defeat—by lies, ignorance, and prejudice—of the progressive forces behind that single line, and with it, of the values that drive ahead human evolution, that again verified what Riane already knew. Legal change was not enough. If change was to come it had to be cultural.

But what kind of cultural change?

Three questions shaped her work. What kind of culture supports equality, justice, and peace? Is such a culture possible? What stands in its way?

To find the answers, she had given up her law practice, we had moved to Carmel, and for ten long years our home became her as well as my research institute.

To keep this chapter reasonably short, at this point I feel torn between what would take another whole book to cover, or going ahead lightly touching on Riane's work, and seeing what happens.

What comes back to me is how during the *Chalice* days—just as we've now recently gone through with her newest book, the typically bold and original probe of *The Real Wealth of Nations*—week by week there piled up in her office and on our shelves books of all the fields she turned to. The phone also seemed constantly engaged with calls to national and international authorities with questions or—in a way that endeared her to a widening circle over the years—to engage in respectful and friendly arguments over matters in dispute. In these ways, she probed history, psychology, sociology, biology, economics, spirituality, and seemingly everything in between to the core.

In particular, she was driven to look at what people believed in and lived by across a wide variety of cultures globally—that is, cross-culturally—and back through history into what came before, the prehistory of the earliest cultures on this earth.

After a decade of burying herself in research, and writing and rewriting draft after draft, and wondering whether anything would ever come of it, she sent the resulting book to the University of California Press. Among those chosen by this scholarly press to be the book's "blind readers"—that is, readers given no knowledge of who had written it—was the great anthropologist Ashley Montagu.

"The most important book since Darwin's *Origin of Species,*" he wrote in his review of the book, which Riane later obtained from the University of California Press.

By then a leading New York literary agent, Ellen Levine, had decided she wanted to represent the book. And so in the end, *The Chalice and the Blade: Our History, Our Future* was published in 1987 by Harper & Row instead.

The Chalice and The Blade starts with a new look at stories of origin. It brings to life the emergence of our species' first great Goddess-worshiping cultures, and their displacement by invasions of hordes of warriors driven by an entirely different view and way of life. It then moves from prehistory to history, culminating with the epochal choice before us: evolutionary breakdown or breakthrough.

The early cultures were distinguished by relative peace, comparative equality of the sexes, and a high degree of creativity. Out of this earlier time emerged all the basic inventions, except those for warfare, upon which today's civilization is built—language, religion, architecture, city planning, writing, music, medicine, the precursor for democratic governance, and so forth. The picture in general is of an economy of abundance for a comfortably settled people enjoying and sharing the advantages of the development of agriculture in the fertile areas of our

David Loye

planet.

By contrast, the invaders were nomads. Bands of horse riding herdsmen, they had become hordes fighting with one another to try to make a living in the inhospitable territory of deserts and harsh climatic situations. In striking point for point difference from the earlier cultures, these horseback cultures were distinguished by a strong-man model of a rigidly male dominant and authoritarian power structure, the worship of fierce Gods, and by creativity almost wholly directed to the development of methods of conquest and stealing from others.

It was Riane's great achievement in this book—as well as in *Sacred Pleasure*, in chapters in books edited by others, and in many formal papers for scientific journals—to show how out of the tension between these two primary models for human society emerged everything we have known since as the history of our species. Identifying one as the *partnership* or *gylanic model* and the other as the *dominator, domination,* or *androcratic model*, she reveals, for example, the tragedy of religion in a new light.

In the case of Christianity, we see how the partnership-oriented life and beliefs of Jesus—emphasizing love, peace, and equality—were converted into the bloody domination drive of the crusades, the inquisition, and witch burnings. We see how the more egalitarian early arrangements for government became rule by kings, emperors, lords, and all the other names for the tyrants of history.

We also see how a primarily dominator-oriented recorded history has swung back and forth between periods of lessening or increasing strength for this grim model of social, political, and economic governance. But then we see how in modern times there has been a rise of organized and effective challenges to traditions of domination—from the 18th century "rights of man" movement to the later abolitionist, women's rights, civil rights, children's rights, economic justice, anti-war, and environmental movements. Perhaps most important, we see why speeding up a global shift to partnership is so urgently needed in our time when the mix of the domination model and nuclear and biological weapons—and other high technologies in service of "the conquest of nature"—threatens our very survival.

We also see something ignored in earlier studies of cultural evolution: how at the core of it all, as Riane's research extensively documents, lies the decisive relation of the male half and the female half of our species. In other words, rather than being "just a women's issue," the character of gender roles and relations is a key matter that profoundly affects a society's cultural values and social institutions across the board.

After publication, *The Chalice and The Blade* became a key book for the discussion groups that led to the emergence of a partnership movement globally. Demand for a guide that might show how to put this forceful new perspective into action led to our joint production of *The Partnership Way: Healing Our Families, Our Communities, and Our World*, published by Harper San Francisco in 1990, reissued by Holistic Education Press in 1998, and now available from the Center for Partnership Studies at www.partnershipway.org.

Sacred Pleasure: Sex, Myth, and the Politics of the Body (Harper San Francisco, 1995) was a rich, multi-chambered expansion for the drama and the color of this new epic picture of our evolution. A work of much original psychology, it is a bold, highly original, and both captivating and scorching look at how the interaction of these two models has shaped our sexual, spiritual, and political lives. The mix of the two models—for example, in the punitive versus loving methods of child raising—is also revealed as a major source of confusion in all areas of our lives.

Next came *Tomorrow's Children: A Blueprint for Partnership Education in the 21st Century* (Westview Press, 2000). Why a book on education? The reason is that of all the ways we try to push ahead through social action, education offers a system *in place*, already financed and staffed at all levels, without having to build everything from scratch, as is usually the case.

Again a work of amazing scope, *Tomorrow's Children* reexamines education from kindergarten through high school and beyond from the partnership perspective. Central I believe to its historic importance and continuing value for parents and educators is how it makes of education an inspiring tree rather than a confusing pile of sticks. Riane takes the uncoordinated and often confusing scatter of education as it presently exists and rebuilds it into a coherent picture using the story of biological and cultural evolution as the new trunk, with subjects ranging from math to art as the leaves for a newly meaningful tree.

Ah, how pallid this account seems, reading back over what I've written, in comparison to what she has touched off in me and in her readers. What beyond the words on the page moves us, I believe—and this wherever we may live on this troubled earth, of whatever color, male as well as female, rich as well as poor—is the trauma of the trampled, wounded, suppressed, flattened, buried love within all of us that, in recognition, responds to the trauma that drove and drives her.

I came to see as a psychologist that the origin for the ills of mind, body, and soul that afflict our species has many theories and many names on this troubled planet. But go to the core of most of what we suffer and what you will find, in one way or another, is the impact of the dominator way of life—and why the trauma driving Riane touches the trauma within all of us.

Considering the mounting threat to the world posed by the terrorism spawned by the dominator way of life of extremist mullah rule in many Muslim nations today, a hopeful sign is that in 2003 *Tomorrow's Children* became the first of Riane's books to be published in Pakistan. Soon after the Urdu edition came out, it was adopted by the Lahore Government College of Education in Pakistan for use in its M.A. in education program. More recently, it has been adopted for new curriculum development by the Montessori Foundation, with an outreach to 5,000 schools internationally.

The drive to put scholarship directly into action, which has distinguished Riane's work, can again be seen in *The Power of Partnership: Seven Relationships That Can Change Your Life*, published by New World Library in 2002. Over the last part of the 20th century, "self-help" became a major category for books. A problem, however, was the prevailing focus on the self as an island with no responsibility to or connection with the rest of the world. Riane designed this book to encourage the vast readership for self-help books to venture out of isolation into social and political action, as well as to show social and political activists that we can't build a better world without laying the foundations for respect for human rights and nonviolence in the formative parent-child and gender relations.

The Power of Partnership provides practical guidelines for moving ahead in the seven basic relationships that shape us and our world. Our relation with ourselves. With our intimate others. Within the workplace and our community. Within our nation. Within a multi-cultural world at large. With nature and the living environment. And finally, with spirituality.

I feel there is no better way of closing this chapter than to provide the vision of the "gylanic" or partnership world with which Riane ends *The Chalice and the Blade*.

> "For above all, this gylanic world will be a world where the minds of children—both girls and boys—will no longer be fettered. It will be a world where limitation and fear will no longer be systematically taught us through myths about how inevitably evil and perverse we humans are. In this world, children will not be taught epics about men who are honored for being violent or fairy tales about children who are lost in frightful woods where women are malevolent witches. They will be taught new myths, epics, and stories in which human beings are good; men are peaceful; and the power of creativity and love—symbolized by the sacred Chalice, the holy vessel of life—is the governing principle.
>
> "For in this gylanic world, our drive for justice, equality, and freedom, our thirst for knowledge and spiritual illumination, and our yearning for love and beauty will at last be freed. And after the bloody detour of androcratic history, both women and men will at last find out what being human can mean."

THIRTEEN
THE WOMEN'S MOVEMENT AND AFRICA

We've been up against the Domination way of life for thousands of years. So how do we finally end this insanity and move from Domination to Partnership?

Some would make the case for the labor movement. Some for the civil rights and human rights movements. Some for a new and improved socialism. Some for a vastly improved capitalism. Whatever else we might push for—if only considering the accelerating consequences of global warming and nuclear overkill—most of us would push for the environmental and peace movements.

For me the women's movement was and remains the most important. Through my association with Riane, I came not only to know and fight for it. I came to see what it brought to all other movements against the domination way of life and how, most fundamentally, this movement advances the partnership way.

What women brought to the fray was a social head of steam that during the 20th century finally boiled over out of 5,000 years of repression. They brought voices, hoarse with shouting and with pleading, to at last open the eyes of a species blinded to the imbalance, illogic, and injustice of this situation. They liberated the drive of mind, heart, and soul toward the balance, logic, and justice of gender equality.

David Loye

It is not that women are better than men by nature. The grim fact is that through being required by the dominator system to fight its bloody battles, to contend with other males hardened to the task, to outwit one another in school, in business, religion, and in every other area of life, the males of our species have been taught to become insensitive to, and even to deny the validity of what at the same time they are taught are humanity's highest ideals.

This basic inconsistency not only produces the dishonesty and hypocrisy of the stereotypical male—and thereby the dishonesty and hypocrisy of the conservatism that by rote has worked fiercely to preserve the endemic disaster of male domination. It has also fueled the paradigm of superior over inferior that underlies war, racism, scientism, environmental degradation, the lust for conquest, and all other dark products of the Dominator Way.

My first plunge into battle came in 1977 when Riane decided she had to write *The Equal Rights Handbook*. This is a story of historical importance, which calls for a closer look.

At that time, passage of The Equal Rights Amendment (or ERA, as it came to be known) to the U.S. Constitution was considered one of the most important issues facing women in the U.S. It had passed in the U.S. House of Representatives 354 to 24, in the Senate 84 to eight. Over 450 national organizations were supporting it, with a combined membership of 50-million. Already it had been ratified by thirty-five states. Only three more ratifications were needed to make it a law that would apply uniformly across the entire nation. Yet like the biblical cloud no bigger than a man's hand along the horizon—out of what up until then was nationally considered the "lunatic fringe"—there rose what in retrospect looms as the pivotal turn backward for America as the right-wing mobilized for holy war.

Behind scenes—as I detail in *Bankrolling Evolution*—a first installment of the billions regressive foundations were to put behind the backward shove were poured into the fight against the ERA by the Coors beer brewing family. A coalition of right wing Catholic and Protestant fundamentalists led by the anti-feminist Phyllis Schlafly rapidly gained size. Over television, radio, and in scores of leaflets and booklets, they hammered across the message that passage of the ERA threatened all that held America together and that God Himself personally valued.

Hearkening to the call that was ultimately to morally bankrupt the party and endanger the world, the Republican party had begun the steady roll to the right that put the anti-ERA president, Ronald Reagan, in office and set the stage for the seizure of all three branches of the American government during the G.W.Bush years.

There was no adequate book on the Equal Rights Amendment to serve as a rallying handbook on social, political, and economic action—that is, how to boycott Coors and other supporters of the anti-ERA campaign, how to lobby for it, how to write letters to editors, and all the other basic tactics used to effectively promote good causes. Realizing that her background in constitutional law and in drafting a brief for the Supreme Court made her one of the few people in the country able to produce what was needed in a hurry, Riane felt obligated to write such a book. But how could it be done in time to be of use? Would I help?

It would be a formidable task within the short time frame for getting it out and into book stores. At the time, it seemed to me, and still does, a case made in heaven, as they say, for joining the skills of two lovers in the production of our joint social activist brainchild. She had the needed legal expertise and feminist credentials. I had the needed fast, breezy, deadline-meeting skill from my earlier years as a journalist, as well as the research, book production and promoting skills required. For four months I lived two lives. In the mornings I was Professor Loye, Research Director of a $500,000 pioneering study of the impact of movies and television on adults. In the afternoons I was an unsung working stiff drawing on my earlier years as a journalist and as an advertising agency account exec—both of which had often entailed feats of research and writing overnight that would have required weeks, months, and even years in academia. And out of this emerged *The Equal Rights Handbook*.

But it was too late. The lies that ERA would destroy marriage and morality and harm rather than help women had taken hold, and legislators in the key states used these lies to vote their prejudices. ERA was defeated.

However, for us the battle was now personally and in tandem joined. We were in it for the long term—and still are.

The most memorable high point for me came with the immense gathering of women from around the world in Nairobi, Kenya, for the United Nations Decade for Women Conference of 1985.

I had not wanted to go originally. Despite my commitment and enthusiasm, the idea of being one of a tiny handful of men in the middle of thousands of women, and the long flight from California to Europe and then to Africa and back, was anything but engaging. But then came a terrorist attack in the region, with increasing reports of the threat of terrorist attacks on the women in Nairobi.

How better to gain world headlines for some insane purpose than by dropping bombs into the global gathering of thousands of hypothetically defenseless women far from home?

I decided I had to go. In mind, I practiced how I would protect Riane. Out of the darkness would step a terrorist, perhaps planning to throw a sack over her and carry her off screaming to hold as a hostage. Swift as that nemesis of evil, The Shadow of my childhood years of being glued to the radio at supper time, I would dart silently upon him and with deft pressure to the right nerve in his neck, render him unconscious and rescue her.

That I was already 60 at the time made the success of such an intervention doubtful, but this in no way watered down my resolve.

From the start, we were swept up and consumed by the energy of this second world conference for half our species—the first had been in Mexico a decade earlier. The clothes, the bodies, the skin colors of all kinds, the rich buzz of hundreds of differing languages, the roaming glances of the gleaming eyes everywhere drinking it in—from all over the world they had come here. In the vast meeting hall, they laughed and shouted at each other, then hushed to hear the speakers, among them the stars of the feminist world. Bella Abzug of the deep voice and great flappy hat. Betty Friedan, looking rather dumpy and frumpy, I thought. And Margarita Papandreou, the very image of the male ideal for women, stately, beautiful, but also, seizing the hunger for power of the women, with the commanding presence of the wife of a head of state.

Riane and her gorgeous blonde friend from Finland, Hillka Pietila, were resplendent in their contributions to the temporarily stilled throng. Symbolic of what was most deeply at move there, however, was the old African woman who stood up out of the audience to speak at one point.

She was clad in rags. Her voice was quivering and her hand was wavering as she clutched a long stick to support herself, struggling to be heard.

The noise was immense, drowning her voice until shouts of "Keep quiet!" "Let her speak!" finally stilled the chamber.

Then in a halting voice, punctuated by the deep and weary intake of her breathing as someone held a microphone close to her mouth so she could be heard, she told her story. She lived in a village out in the desert away from Nairobi, the translator reported. They had little water and could raise barely enough crops to stay alive. There had been a school once for the children, but now it was gone. It was hard for the men too, but hardest for the women, for they were treated as no better than beasts by the men.

"I heard there is a big meeting in Nairobi. They said it is something that can not be believed. They said this is a meeting for women from far away who have the power of chiefs. They will meet and talk, and maybe something good will happen for us. Maybe for our village. Maybe for the children. Maybe everywhere."

The giant chamber was still. All eyes were on her. You could feel the emotion rolling like a wave through the assembled thousands of women from all lands, East, West, North, South.

"I walked fifty miles," she cried out.

"With my stick."

She shook it before her.

"I want to see with my eyes if this is true."

That weekend we saw where she had come from—but from the haunting perspective of three days so radically different from what she had year after year known, and day after day would know for the rest of her life. Signing up for a safari, we flew in a light plane out over the brown and mystic majesty of the Great Rift Valley to the game preserve

3,000 Years of Love

of Masai Mara.

The old woman lived somewhere down below us in the tiny villages that dotted the dry, brown, seemingly endless and barren expanse of land. We could see the bony cattle. The stray pig or two. A woman here and there with a jug balanced on her head, setting out to get water from out there where no patch of green was showing—out in that brown stretch where, blinking for comfort, one felt one's eyes going dry just looking at it. Down there, literally scratching for a living. With each day a question about next day's food and fuel.

By contrast, here we were, like the white gods of this earth empowered to soar through the air, untouched, above it all. Here we were, after landing, housed among the lush forests of Masa Mara in luxurious camps of squeaky clean beds and sumptuous meals. Here we were, cared for from waking in the morning to going to sleep at night by eager smiling black attendants, with everything else one could wish for.

Hiring a jovial, intelligent, and movie-star handsome black guide with an open top jeep, we set out through the grass. It was waist high in all directions. Swishing past us like waves on either side, to cut through the high grass in this jeep was like speeding through the water in a boat reveling in its wild and carefree power.

A herd of zebra appear, their gait nervous, their stripes blurring into a sensation of seeing them slanting through the grass.

Giraffes are rocking heads on the rocking necks that is all you can see of them in the distance rising out of the grass.

We come on the brooding immensity of a herd of elephants—with the guide's explanation he can go no nearer, as with babies to protect among them they are liable to charge. Then comes the nonchalance of a family of lions sprawled on a rock—with the guide from long experience driving up to within 15 feet of them without the flicker of so much of an eyelash on their part.

Perhaps most striking of all, out there in the African wild, was the astonishing sky of a size I still cannot understand. In all directions it stretched upward and outward to fill the space from the dark ring of the horizons like no other skies I have seen on this earth.

Then there were the sunsets to exhaust all words of superlatives—like the symphonic interweaving of the red, the blue, the purple and the gold in paintings by the great English painter Turner, if Turner had been more than a mortal, more like a Goddess or God.

Most memorable of all was the annual migration of the wildebeest from the plains of the Serengeti across the raging Grumeti river from Tanzania into Kenya, which we luckily were just in time to witness.

There before us was the seemingly endless jogging mass. By current count this was the surge of *two million* wildebeest on the move.

According to African legend, the wildebeest were made by the gods out of spare parts left over after assembling the other animals. With outsize nodding heads on what by comparison seem spindly legs, they came thundering down into the water on the far side of the river. For a stretch each became a desperate head in the gasping, snorting, struggling mass, then they re-emerged on our side, to fight among themselves to clamber up the bank and to join the swell of black wet backs that filled the land on past us, lumbering on and on as far as eye could see.

It was like the flow of the life force on exuberant display. All in all, the land, the forests, the sky, the animals in this their natural setting—to be there was like being in at the beginning. To be back millions of years "before man." To be back shortly after some biblical creation.

3,000 Years of Love

One might say it was a crazy notion, but at the same time I somehow feel it wasn't crazy—to feel that we were back in a time of primal innocence when one might start all over and do it better this time.

Back in Nairobi to finish the conference we were approached by Riane's friend Nikki Beare and a small, thin, elfin woman with brisk movements and caustic funny remarks whose name we learned was Susanna Downnie

Nikki Beare was one of those people who immediately put you at ease with the feeling here is someone you can trust. A past national president of NOW, she had a public relations and travel agency in Miami. Part of the time she booked tours from it and the rest of the time she lobbied for good causes or worked for good candidates in the Florida legislature.

I think of her now—that touch of memory in my life of so many of those people in the lives of all of us. Those whom we met, wish we could have known longer or more of, yet who whisk in and out of our lives leaving only the later flicker in the mind that for a minute or so brightens one's thoughts and then is gone again.

Their problem was this, Nikki told us. They were housed in a small complex of motels designated for the press. But what they soon found was that everything seemed to have been deliberately arranged to make it almost impossible for anyone in the independent press without special connections or privileges—that is, under control of the authorities—to function. In the whole complex, there was but a single pay telephone, presumably to be fought over around the clock by journalists trying to get something of what was going on out to the outside world.

Officially this incredible situation was being fobbed off by the Kenyans as a case of someone's goof, so sorry. But to anyone who knew anything about the press and its function in a free society it was obvious this seemingly tiny detail served to effectively throttle its voice. In view of much more of this sort of thing later faced by women and journalists without inner sanctum blessing during the next U.N. Decade for Women Conference in Beijing in 1995, it's evident the press situation wasn't coincidental.

Both Kenya and China were essentially dictatorships rigidly run from the top down. Thus they shared the same strategic problem in taking on what must have seemed to the leadership the nightmare mixed blessing of these huge gatherings of women and journalists from all over the world. On one hand, they were eager for the money this would bring into the country. On the other hand, they were scared sockless of what those who were not under the official thumb might write about them.

"I know it's an awful thing to ask, but could we possibly use the telephone in your hotel room to send out our reports?" Nikki asked.

We were staying in the New Stanley Hotel. It was named after New York Herald Tribune reporter Henry Stanley. Gaining global fame by journeying into the heart of darkest Africa to find the explorer Dr. David Livingstone, it was Stanley who passed on to posterity the deathless phrase, "Dr. Livingstone, I presume?"

I see on checking for a picture on the internet that the "New" has been dropped and a $20-million face lift and tummy tuck has since converted it into what happens to hotels of charm these days. But thank goodness, to me The New Stanley Hotel will always remain suitably embellished by memory's comfortable distortions. I will forever see it as that wonderful, rambling old British colonial structure, replete with the wide porches, fancy scrollwork, and even the romantic turrets with flags flying of the Victorian age.

3,000 Years of Love

"We will just be in and out once a day. As I say, we don't want to be any trouble," Nikki added anxiously as Riane delayed an answer.

"I certainly want to be helpful. Let's see how it goes," Riane said—and so began the saga of how the four of us launched the Women's International Network News Syndicate, a world first of its kind. Nikki and Susanna became the Editors of its International Edition. Riane and I became the first of the dozen or so reporters that Nikki and Susanna recruited from among the women there. Our job was to seek out and write stories on everything that the Kenyan officials or the international press lords would prefer to see ignored.

It soon became apparent that these old hands at bucking the system knew what they were up to and had come well prepared. No sooner did we open our room to them than Susanna pounced on the telephone, unhooked it from the wall outlet, and pulled from her knapsack a contraption I had never seen before. This proved to be a first generation, hot-off-the-shelf electronic device with a typewriter keyboard. Ostensibly, this early precursor of the computer and internet revolution would allow you to plug the device into a phone line at one end and then type in and transmit whatever you wished to be picked up again elsewhere in the form of a printed rather than voice message. Susanna swiftly typed in a brief message, then stood up and smiled at us.

"We'll have to wait now. In fact, we might do well to go get something to eat and come back."

Grinning and relishing what they had to impart to us, over dinner she and Nikki sketched out the full picture of what, if all worked, had now been set in motion.

From here in the outwardly disarming innocence of our room in the New Stanley in Nairobi, the message had gone over the phone and long-buried under-sea trans-Atlantic lines to merry old England to let London know the beachhead for our secret mission was secure with electronic super-tool now in place and functional. At the London end co-conspirators were now, while we dined, executing the next step.

In London, there was a new kind of free access, public facility, established through Labor Party diligence, which piped up messages to a satellite that circled the Earth for transmission anywhere in the world. From "our woman" or women in London, our first message and all succeeding reports would shoot out from earth over 22,000 miles through space to the satellite and from there back down to the office of the Executive Editor of this ad hoc new global syndicate. In this case, operating after-hours in the quiet secrecy of the night, it was another woman who in day time officialdom was Managing Editor of the prestigious *Louisville Courier* in Kentucky.

This was the route that all our news reports would go on out to reach a hypothetical world readership, Nikki explained. For a questionnaire had been sent out to key newspapers in the U.S. and abroad to sign up all those who might be interested in this feminist counter-culture coverage as an alternative to the mainstream press's focus on Palestinian-Israeli encounters and other "politics as usual" dispatches.

Our reports focused on the ideas, needs, and aspirations of women worldwide that were dismissed and ignored by the press. Working into the night with her recruited local collaborators, the *Louisville Courier* editor was set up to transmit our reports to all who had signed up for this pioneering global service.

Suitably awed, Riane and I marveled over the ingenuity of this hookup. The more one thought about it, the more it raised in mind a sort of wild tinker-toy, or the kind of goofy, home-spun contraption for which the cartoonist Rube Goldberg or Dr.Seuss were famous—the gizmo here in the African hotel bedroom, the mystic junction in London, the multi-billion dollar satellite circling the Earth, the band of women secretly working into the night out of the Kentucky newspaper office.

We set to work and soon our hotel room became a miniature Grand Central Station through which daily, and at odd hours through the night, in and out there trouped the four of us and other recruited reporters to type out our stories on the gizmo with the keyboard by the phone jack. We all laughed together a bit over our somewhat comical situation, until one day there was a knock at the door.

Answering it, I found a grim-faced black man in trim Western business suit.

"I am the house detective. The Front Desk says there's something funny going on with your phone," he said, trying to peer past me into the room. "I wonder if I might take a look at it."

"Why of course," I said. "Come in and have a look."

This was a safe bet, for in order not to raise wonderment and gossip among the maids we detached and hid the gizmo when not in use, replugging the phone to allay suspicions. He looked, tried the phone, and shook his head.

He grinned apologetically.

"Those people, they get the craziest ideas sometimes," he said, nodding in the general direction of the Front Desk.

If we had been found out, it could have had grave consequences. We could have landed in a Kenyan jail for who knows how long. But the sheer fun of feeling that, against the odds, we might be beating the Domination system, overrode all fears.

For Riane and me, the climax came with a scene that could have fitted into a Marx Brothers movie. On the other side of our bed, close to the wall, Nikki's elfin friend was huddled over the gizmo, typing feverishly. On our bed Nikki and another reporter were seated with yellow tablets writing out stories in long-hand to pass on to her. Another reporter had our one chair.

To find some place to sit down, as well as to gain the quiet and privacy we both needed to finish our stories, Riane and I retreated to the bathroom with the door shut. She seated herself on the toilet cover and began writing. I looked around, and as there was no other place to sit, climbed into the bathtub, made myself comfortable, and hand printed out my story for the day.

It was impossible later to find out how many of our stories got through "enemy lines" and were printed, or where they might have appeared. After getting back to the States, however, I quickly discovered the wisdom of the venture.

Typically, the mainstream wire service coverage of this pivotal event for that year was just plain disgusting. The reporters sanctioned by the press overlords, with the mainstream editors back home dutifully punching up the message with their headlines, had pounced on every little bit of dissension and division to portray the event as if it was merely a bunch of fish-wives stridently haggling over a table arrangement, or hens clucking and clacking over who gets the morsel of corn in a farmyard.

The clash of Israeli with Palestinian women, for example, was the big news for the world out of the conference for one day. Riane and I were there. The purpose of the panel that purportedly was the source for this story was to bring women from both sides together to discuss how they might work together to bring peace to the Middle East. While

3,000 Years of Love

Riane and I watched and listened, the statements and the discussion both ways were thoughtful and mutually respectful throughout almost the whole of the panel. Then it was briefly interrupted by a group of Palestinian women who angrily marched in to disrupt the meeting, but were soon edged out and the discussion went on peacefully and respectfully as before.

It was a single isolated incident, as if on a sunny day one cloud briefly appeared. Yet to the world at large, "Palestinian women clash with Israeli women" was the big news about the UN Women's Conference for that day!

Soon afterward there also began to appear in major national magazines and newspapers articles with titles like Is Feminism Dead? Beyond Feminism. Feminism and Other Passing Fads. The chest-thumping macho posturing of poet Robert Bly steadily gained more columns in the magazines. Concomitantly, the coverage for the anti-feminist diatribes of Camille Paglia and others of this ilk took off.

These and the swarm of other attempts to dig the grave and bury the women's movement were documented by Susan Faludi in *Backlash*, a brilliant expose of the dynamics of dominator systems regression for which Riane's work provides the cultural, historical, and evolutionary analysis.

What Riane and I and thousands of women from all over the world had personally witnessed and experienced in Nairobi had been anything but the end of feminism. The real news was that here—of major potential impact for the history and evolution of our species—we had witnessed a bonding of women of all colors worldwide at both the official and the grassroots leadership levels, from a majority of the nations of the world, across a wide variety of religions, languages, and cultural beliefs.

Here had been a major reaffirmation of feminism and the hope for humanity that had characterized the earlier UN Decade for Women Conference in Mexico City in 1975, that was again to occur in the Beijing UN Women's Conference in 1995, both of which were similarly warped and distorted via transmission to the outside world by the servile and fallen angels of the press.

Behind the new words coined to undermine and discredit the movement—such as "Women's Lib," "Fem-Lib" and "Feminnazi"—was nothing less than an attempt to halt and if possible wipe from the planet this most powerful and most peaceful of all revolutions.

FOURTEEN
OF THE HYDRA AND GREECE

When I think of all the places to which Riane and I journeyed to share ideas with others from around the world on how to counter what we're up against, I find the image of Hercules battling the Hydra comes to mind.

The Hydra was the multi-snake-headed monster the hero had to fight in the Greek legend of the Labors of Hercules. The problem was that as soon as Hercules bashed in one head with his club, another would grow in its place, and so the monster became stronger rather than weaker until Hercules found a way to overcome it.

What's forgotten today, most significantly, is that Hercules didn't do it alone. He had partners. In all the battles and trials of ingenuity of the famous twelve labors of Hercules it was often the intervention of the goddess Athena, the god Hermes, or his trusty nephew Iolaus that tipped the scale in his favor.

I had taken on the Hydra head of racism in my first book, *The Healing of a Nation*. Then Riane and I met, and sexism became the Hydra head. To learn from and share with others involved with the women's movement, we journeyed to Greece, Germany, Spain, France, and Kenya—as well as for Riane alone, to Sweden, Russia, Argentina, Costa Rica, Brazil, Columbia, Canada, Chile, and many other places.

David Loye

We journeyed to Hungary, Italy, Austria, Croatia, and Finland to battle the Hydra head of a PseudoDarwinian scientism and other Hydras of the domination system. And in the lonely battle, over what in retrospect seems an inconceivable number of years, I fought the Hydra head of moral insensitivity.

It is the multiple heads of the Hydra that year after year capture the attention and energy of most of us who decry them, write about them, and take and urge others to take action against them. But behind the heads we sought to find and reveal the body of the monster. For apparent to us and to increasing numbers of those we met within the tiny gatherings of the concerned and often best informed of people on the planet, and in all the conferences and symposia we attended, were two new heads the monster was sprouting: environmental devastation and nuclear overkill. So again and again the tocsin sounded, or muffled still reached us subliminally: that unless a way could be found to end the reign of the Hydra the human experiment on this earth was doomed.

Rather than the old image of the Hydra, however—which poses difficulties besides the bashing in of heads when one looks into the original story—we worked to seed a new story that can take us beyond all the Hydras if we work together. We focused on the two positive symbols of hope that run through our work: the Flame for me, and the Chalice for Riane.

Because of its pivotal place in the 35,000 year stretch for human evolution that Riane covers in *The Chalice and the Blade,* the Greek island of Crete was a place for us of great meaning.

To see Greece for the first time was of course enormously exciting. To speed through the Greek islands on a giant hydrofoil and see these rocks encrusted with whole towns and villages emerge blinding white out of the deepest blue of the sea. To look out from the window of our hotel in Athens and see the Parthenon really there high on the hill across from us. To hear the wailing thrum of the bazouki and watch the sinuous movement of the dancers toeing, flashing, and flowing to this wild music in the night clubs. But to at last see the ancient ruins of Minoan Crete itself was beyond excitement.

As a Boy Scout in Oklahoma roaming the Osage Hills, I had first known this special feeling. There is something elemental in the thrill of unexpectedly finding for oneself an arrowhead, or a potsherd, or any other ancient artifact. Seeing the remains of the Minoan palace of Knossos is this—multiplied many times over.

To begin with, it is not at all what one expects after seeing the ruins of ancient civilizations elsewhere—or even our own cities into fairly recent times. Knossos was startling in its modernity. It is situated on a green hillside selected to maximize its relation to the sun for cooling in summer and heat in winter. Its levels and rooftops are a series of clean ascending planes supported by the tasteful punctuation of row on row of scarlet columns. The structure has the look of something far more intelligent in its layout than prevailed for thousands of years after this complex was destroyed by earthquake and fire around 1450 B.C.E.

It was here over four thousand years ago, from about 2600 to 1200 B.C.E., on Crete and on its now tiny nearby neighbor, the island of Thera, or Santorini as it is known today, that the great early culture of what is known as Minoan Civilization flourished. It is here that scholars speculate the real life Atlantis that Plato wrote about flowered until it was destroyed.

From geological and historical evidence, we know today that rather than being some mystic land that long ago sank beneath the Atlantic ocean, as is still a popular notion, Atlantis seems to have been this ancient civilization, with the legend of its sinking deriving from the volcanic explosion that obliterated and sank much of nearby Santorini. We know, too, from the evidence of the hundreds of studies Riane drew on for *The Chalice and the Blade:* that Minoan Crete was the site of a high point for the earlier more peaceful and highly creative partnership-oriented culture that was over-run and displaced by the violent and destructive "dominator" culture that has mashed, mangled, and bloodied the history of our species on this planet ever since.

We had come to Crete as emissaries of the new partnership movement then erupting through the spread around the U.S. of small discussion/action groups following publication of *The Chalice and the Blade* in 1987, and then into the larger world with publication of the book's foreign editions. We were meeting with the wife of the Prime Minister and first lady of Greece, Margarita Papandreou, with the Mayor of Heraklion and other dignitaries about the possibility of a first international conference of the partnership movement. Then in the talking and planning stage, the hope for all of us was that this event could be a kind of "home coming" to draw partnership-minded people from around the world to Crete as an early home for this new present day ideal.

Here we could see the palace at Knossos not flat on the page in a book but looking at the real thing. Within the ruins of the building, and in the museums loaded with its artifacts, we were seeing what was difficult to believe even with our own eyes. The tiny figurines and wall paintings of bare-breasted priestesses or goddesses bespoke of religious power for women. Rather than kneeling or groveling before some fearful God who may strike one dead at any time, as is found into our day, the clay figure of a male worshipper stands there proud and upright. Shoulders thrust back, he looks upward with the back of his clasped right hand clapped to his forehead in a dignified salute to the deity.

There is the perfect head of a bull carved out of black steatite with gilded horns. The thousands of seals carved of agate and other semiprecious stones—revealing much of the difference for this culture, each a marvel of originality was worn on a strap around the wrist by Minoans, I'm personally convinced, to assert their individuality. In other words, I believe (though of course cannot prove) that as today we wear a wrist watch binding us together in a worldwide uniformity of time, they wore these seals that as a routine, everyday matter, proclaimed that they saw themselves as well as others as unique, each something special—rather than just one of the peons or the mob who were despised and exploited by their rulers elsewhere already then throughout the known world.

The guide books call the sites in Knossos and the lesser ruins in Phaistos, Malia, Zakros, Archanes, and Gournia "palaces." This is an interesting indication of the degree to which our perceptions of and words for things are automatically captive of the dominator paradigm. To call them "palaces" is dictated by what almost everywhere else the giant main structures serving as residence and fortress for the Kings and Queens of early times are called. But scholars—such as the Greek archeologist Nicholas Platon, the former head of the Acropolis Museum who excavated Crete over 50 years—have uncovered something else entirely. They have shown that these "palaces" actually served as large multi-purpose religious, administrative, manufacturing, distribution, and dwelling centers.

These findings are typically ignored or glossed over by many academics and writers of popular books—like millions of us still unconsciously enslaved, still driven to serve the prevailing paradigm.

There were chambers that did indeed serve as the residence of the leaders. In the case of Minoan Crete—reminding me of the peace chiefs and the war chiefs of the Indian tribes I knew in my Oklahoma days—the leaders appear to have been priestesses coupled with some form of complementary male leadership, perhaps from the Minoan merchant fleet plying the Mediterranean and for national defense.

But these "palaces" also served as centers for religion, with chambers for religious ceremonies and quarters for priestesses and priests. They also served as the factories of that time—that is, as centers for the crafts, jewelry, pottery, weaving, etc. They also served as both the centralized warehouse for the storage of olive oil, grains, and other foodstuffs, and as a distribution center, perhaps for a kind of supermarket of that time.

As for the gulf historically separating "the two halves of humanity," as Riane has often put it, the domination of male over female, or the sexism undermining practically every area of our lives still rampant throughout most of world even today is striking in its absence. In the bull leaping that was a favorite ritual and spectator sport, for example, can be found evidence of the prevailing ethos of partnership between women and men.

How it worked was like this. As duplicated in modern times, you ran at a charging bull, seized the horns with both hands as if riding a bicycle—and then impelled by the power of the startled thrust upward of the bull's head were catapulted into the air, ideally somersaulting, to lightly land beyond the bull to the cheers of the crowd.

It's widely believed the bulls for this ritual were raised from calfhood to adulthood, hence were somewhat tamed, but were still formidable beasts, symbolizing the power of nature.

The most famous Minoan mural is of an enormous red bull and three bull-leapers. All wear only a loin cloth. But where elsewhere all three would be male, with the female relegated to the sidelines, or sexually obliterated within some equivalent of the Islamic burka of today, in this case the two at either end of the bull are female and the one flying through the air over the bull is a male. It is as bold an assertion in art of gender equality as one is likely to find anywhere in history.

Not only was there no evidence of the putdown of one gender by the other. To the contrary, everywhere we looked could be found a frank, open, sensuous, and uninhibited reveling in and valuing of sexual difference. In the paintings and the figurines of women, the breasts are saucily thrust forth from clothing designed for their display. The width and curve to the hips was emphasized. For women their hair-dos were not only strikingly modern but set off with the enticement of the deliberately wild strand of hair here and there, or the "teasing," in high fashion today. As for the men, again the emphasis on open sexuality came through in the bulge to the loin cloth indicating where the genitals are.

Perhaps most haunting of all was what we have at last come to see and value in our time, when all about us loom the environmental consequences of the escalating billions of our species who seem hellbent on trashing this very rare planet and all life on it. Everywhere we looked in Knossos, and on the island of Santorini and other Minoan sites, could be seen the evidence of a greater love for and valuing of nature than in anywhere else in all of antiquity, with the exception of two brief early Egyptian dynasties.

In other words, where the art elsewhere was practically wall to wall celebration of war and killing, here were the remnants of murals and carved jewels celebrating the beauty of plants and animals of every kind—blue dolphins leaping from the water, bees at work, antelope at play, lilies gracefully marching along borders, two hovering swallows who seem to be kissing each other.

All in all—in the feeling for the intrinsic as well as decorative beauty of animals and plants, and in other touches asserting a love of life, appreciation of gender differences, and open valuing of sex—it seemed to me we were looking at the explosion out of prehistory of a flowering of our species that exhibited an astonishing degree of equality and freedom for so ancient a time.

Seeing all this and more on our several trips to Greece and Crete had a profound and lasting effect on us. It is no coincidence that Riane designed—and at what seemed to me an astronomical cost—had that awful kitchen in our home rebuilt into an evocation of the colors, the look, and even the friendly, nurturant, prohuman feeling of Minoan Crete.

Seeing with our own eyes—and walking through the ruins, able to touch the sacred stones and look out and see the same land *they* had seen—has made all the difference. To see this evidence that we do have this capacity for the partnership rather than the dominator way within our nature has helped to shore us up to go on whenever it looked like there was nothing to do but despair.

Year after year since then, Minoan Crete has served to remind us and by now many others that it pays to persist in the fight for the better world—rather than bury oneself in trivia in order to avoid looking at what so many of us, and so much of what passes for life today, have become.

I sought to capture some of this in this poem written the day after a trip to one of the most meaningful places on the island—the Lasithi plateau, a wide flat and fertile land hidden high in the mountains, which served as a refuge during the final years of Minoan independence.

To Lasithi

Higher and higher the bus ascended, the valleys
on either side deepening into shadow, until
far below we saw the houses small as pebbles
along the beach and the blue, blue sea beyond.
Still higher, ahead and far above awaited the
sentinel ruins, once windmills, their blocky
bodies and the ancient shattered arms dark
against the veiled haze of a Cretan summer sky.
Then soon the road cut upward through the
pass and with the sense of a celestial elevator
at last halting we were over the top and
looking down into the wide wonder of the Lasithi
plateau spreading out before us mile upon mile
within the dark circle of the mountains' arms.

Here once they hid from the invaders, here no
more than a few miles away but high here where
from below no one could suspect there was this
bowl of plenty, these fields of grain, these
olive groves, these goats lazily grazing,
these looms at work, the dancing, the singing,

(continued)

David Loye

the old love, the true love shared, and the
great, cool, dark, deep cave, alight now with our
torches, alive now with the echoing voices, with
the chanting, where the great Goddess dwelled.

Such is our love now, dearest of all through
eternity. Leaving the crawling, cluttered, maimed
and blinded lowlands world of the invaders far below
now, we have reached this place—the high, high
plateau of our love, this protected land of plenty, from
where we can, as night falls, and the moon rises, sit
together on a high rock, the warm wind touching us
lightly, the gentlest touch of love, the night alive with
the voices of both the living and the beloved dead,
and as the sea calls up to us from far below, see the
future in all its immensity.

Oh world that carries us in this wondrous
womb in time! Can you sense our gratitude?
Can you hasten the time of the gathering of
all of us here on the high plateau, with the
night of love going on forever, and the day
an endless song?

FIFTEEN
THE GERG ADVENTURE

It began with the flavor and suspense of a spy movie.

"This is Istvan Kiss," the deep voice with the heavy Slavic accent said on the phone. "I'm calling from Budapest."

The year was 1984. The U.S. and the Soviet Union were still in the throes of the Cold War. A call from behind the Iron Curtain signaled something potentially dangerous but intriguing.

I confirmed I was indeed the Dr. Loye he was calling. He then explained he was calling on the behalf of Ervin Laszlo, whom I knew only at the time to be one of those international eminences who gave keynote addresses to important meetings and other large gatherings to address the world's problems.

"Professor Laszlo has asked me to invite you to join us here in Budapest next month for an important, high-level gathering of experts."

What was the nature of the meeting, I asked. Kiss said that he was not at liberty to explain its exact nature, but that it would be small, private, involving about twelve to fifteen scientists interested in chaos theory, at that time just coming into vogue internationally. These experts, he emphasized, would be coming from both sides of the Iron Curtain, from Harvard among other places in the U.S., and from the leading think tank on science and social policy in Russia, as well as from

David Loye

Hungary's oldest and most prestigious university.

Why was I being invited? What was my expected contribution?

Embarrassed, Kiss explained he really didn't know as he wasn't acquainted with my work. All he knew was that Professor Laszlo insisted that I be contacted and urged to attend with, of course, all travel and expenses paid. He was also at liberty to say that if our initial three day meeting at Budapest was successful, we would journey on as a group to Vienna for a special presentation to the Director General of one of the most important international scientific agencies.

This was, Kiss stressed again, a meeting of potentially critical importance during this critical time in East-West relations, with both sides having accumulated enough nuclear missiles to wipe out a good part of the earth if their mutual fear and animosity was triggered into war.

I was, by now, thoroughly sold on the idea, however mysterious, and greatly excited by the prospect. But I realized that this was likely to be just another one of those well-intentioned scientific meetings where male eminences and other male experts sat around a table rehashing the same old stuff that had got us nowhere in the past.

Through experience and my reading of such gatherings, the image by then formed in my mind was of a bunch of apes gathered in a jungle to take turns pounding their chests to signal their own importance and the importance of the same old ideas to one another. Having become engaged in the women's movement, aware of its revolutionary importance and of the fresh, renewing stream of scholarship inspired by it such as Riane's work, I immediately felt this was what was needed to interrupt the ritual pounding of the bestial chest.

Championing the full humanistic vision—that is, a vision driven by the equality of both halves of humanity in all areas of life and mind—yes, unquestionably this was what was needed to end what all too often had proved to be the automaton march of male science to another war, or another Holocaust or Hiroshima.

I explained to Kiss I would be delighted to come and that my partner had a revolutionary new work and perspective that would be vital to consider if breakthrough policies were to be explored.

Though I feared—and sadly felt sure—that I was endangering my own chances of going by doing this, I told Kiss that I felt that hers would be the more important contribution and I would be glad to come if she might be included.

Sure enough, they met without me. I thought that was that. But soon I got another call, this time from Professor Laszlo himself. He explained they had met but without completing their vital task or the journey on to Vienna. He was calling to again urge me to a new meeting of the same core group in Budapest.

He explained he particularly wanted me there because he was an enthusiastic reader of my book *The Sphinx and the Rainbow*, which explored the use of our brain and mind in probing the future. He was aware of my other books and my UCLA School of Medicine credentials. Particularly because of my rare gift for writing that could make science come to life, which would be crucial at this stage, he wanted to personally urge me to come to this meeting to help draft the proposal they would take to Vienna.

Again I said I would be enormously delighted to come, but again stressed that the best contribution I thought I could make would be to bring Riane along and again explained the nature and significance of her new work.

"But none of the rest of us are bringing our wives," Laszlo said.

She wasn't my wife, I explained, for we weren't then married. Technically, she was merely a particularly gifted colleague with an important new perspective to offer.

Could I somehow reach him with what seemed to me the quite accurate historical perspective? If not the politics of at least the token representation. She would be the only woman at a meeting, I pointed out, that, if it was as potentially important as it seemed to be, it was essential that at least one member of half the species should be represented, particularly one with such an important contribution to make.

Again, I figured I had cut my own throat, but was pleasantly surprised to get a call from Istvan Kiss, this time inviting both of us.

From the moment our plane landed in Budapest, I felt we had passed not only from one side to the other of the Iron Curtain. Increasingly, we seemed to be moving out of humdrum, everyday reality onto the set of an Orson Wells movie, most specifically "The Third Man" starring Wells as the mysterious Harry Lime amid the tinkling of the cymbalim and the haunting "Third Man" Theme. We were housed in a giant structure on a barren hill that seemed to have been constructed during the Soviet occupation as a center for rest and recuperation for deserving workers. Both inside and out it had all the style and charm of a 1930s refrigerator, but was clean and the food was good.

Early the next morning we were whisked down the lonely hill on which this structure stood, into the massive murk of Budapest. It was a grim and cloudy day. The building in which we were meeting had once apparently asserted the architectural grandeur of the 19th century Austro-Hungarian Empire, but was now grimy and shabby with the look of long time neglect. We gathered for our meeting around a large, heavy oak table within a small cavern of a room under the sickly light of a single bare light bulb, which gave to our assembled faces a sinister look while deepening the darkness of the pool of shadow surrounding us.

Along our side of the table a man, who I later learned was from Harvard, seemed to be making some feeble attempt at humor to a companion. On the other side of the table, a short, black bewhiskered man, who looked to me like a cartoon of the supposed bomb-throwing anarchist, was snickering while a tall, thin companion whispered in his ear.

We sat there in an uncomfortable silence, with no one bothering to introduce anybody to anybody else, until at last—as if materialized out of the shadow—Professor Laszlo appeared suddenly among us. Soon now the mood shifted to one of a bright expectancy as Laszlo began to outline the mission and his hopes for it.

Laszlo was a thin, wiry man with a face that was both boyish and portentous. Below the eyes one was swiftly attracted to the shaven youthfulness of chin and cheek and the engaging charm of a smile that frequently punctuated the well-constructed and smooth flow of what he had to say. Above this, however, loomed two large brooding eyes beneath heavy eyebrows and a high forehead ringed with an unruly wreath of the pale receding hair that emphasized the gravity and import of what he had to impart to us.

What he had to say at length boiled down to one of the two or three most bold and exciting visions I was to personally encounter during the 20th century.

The idea, in essence, was this. We were meeting here in Budapest at a time when the future for our species hung on the balance, Laszlo said, with our fate potentially to be sealed according to whether the scale was tipped one way or the other. The United States on the West and the Soviet Union on the East were armed with enough nuclear weapons to end civilization with the triggering of another war, with indeed the planet itself at risk if the rate of arms escalation and hostility continued.

As if this weren't bad enough in itself, the dream of a greater future set off by the 18th century enlightenment, mounting during the 19th century, seemed everywhere to be unraveling in social, economic, and political chaos. The population explosion of unchecked birth, the polluting of land, air, and water and everything else pointed toward monumental environmental disaster. This and the developmental disparities between the so-called developed and the Third World countries were moving toward the explosion point.

In this situation, it seemed to Laszlo that the new field of chaos theory, if coupled to an updating and advance for evolution theory, might possibly provide answers for how science and enlightened social policy might save us from the ultimate disaster. Our challenge, working together as scientists in secret from East and West, was to design a project and advance in theory, which might be used to guide us through the chaos of our time to the humanistic order of a greater future and new hope for the 21st century.

He had drawn us together to visualize and draft a proposal for a research project to this end. At the end of this second meeting we would indeed venture on as a group to Vienna and present our proposal to the Director General of the International Institute for Applied Systems Analysis, known as IIASA, for consideration for major funding.

This organization had been formed by Western and Eastern bloc countries to house and fund experts working on global problems they shared in common, for example, problems of optimizing transportation, water, energy, agriculture, and other non-ideological basic concerns. If the project was funded, we would all gain a unique opportunity to advance our own ideas and projects to this end.

And so began what within two years became the General Evolution Research Group, or GERG as we called it, for the acronym that was necessary if you wanted to be taken seriously.

As time went by, GERG grew into a very loose, informal alliance of 48 scientists from a wide range of nations and academic disciplines. Biologists, physicists, psychologists, economists, historians, and systems scientists, we came together intermittently from Italy, France, Germany, England, Finland, and the U.S. from the "free" world, and from the unfree-at-first-but-soon-to-be-freed world of Hungary and Russia.

Nothing came of our journey on to Vienna and our first great plan to save the world—quite a story in itself, I will say, which I want to write of elsewhere. But out of that original meeting came the magnificent idea to which Riane and I—along with persisting others—have devoted our lives.

It is, simply stated, to put the disastrous mindset of "survival of the fittest" and "selfish genes" behind us and build the positive kind of action-oriented theory and story of human evolution that our species must have if it is to prevail, even quite possibly to survive the 21st century, and attain the future that generation after generation of our species over 100,000 years now have dreamed of.

Taking off from Laszlo's pioneering work in this direction, our stated original goal for GERG was to build a theory of *general evolution*—that is, a theory of evolution not just restricted to the cosmic or biological level, as was the case with the NeoDarwinian old model theory that prevailed throughout the 20th century. What we sought to build was an action-oriented general theory of evolution that drew upon the work of *all* fields of science.

It was to be a new model theory that beyond a base in biology ascended into all the higher levels and activities that in fact had shaped the evolution of our species over 100,000 years. It would embrace and provide a new structure for the drive of psychological, cultural, political, economic, technological, and moral and spiritual evolution. To this end we periodically met in a wonderful assortment of places around the world to share papers in formal symposia and thoughts over coffee and dinners and colorful "nights on the town."

Our meeting in Florence, Italy, was the first big one, in tandem with the Club of Rome and the United Nations University. Thereafter, ever so often it was off to Finland, to Austria, to Germany, to Italy, and again to Hungary.

Perhaps the single most exciting of these gatherings was when we GERGites furnished the central attraction for a symposium to celebrate the 900th anniversary of the world's oldest university, the University of Bologna, replete with velvet red programs with gold printing and embossing and other touches proclaiming a time of times.

We also had, and still have I'm thankful to say, our own journal, *World Futures: The Journal of General Evolution*—which over the years has offered a rare refuge for the work of hundreds of scientists throughout the world trying to develop something better than the mainstream offering throughout the 20th century.

The problem with the mainstream theory and story of human evolution was this. And I must stress this problem persisted not only throughout the whole of the 20th century. It still rules the roost for science and society in the 21st century. For what filled and still fills most textbooks, and most of the trade books sold in book stores, which reach the bulk of general readers, presents an uninspiring, degrading, woefully inadequate, and often disastrous picture of who we are, can be, and should be.

Our species, either directly stated or implied, is depicted as primarily driven by ruthless selfishness—by "survival of the fittest." Evolution, it's said, has no more direction or meaning than a pinball set loose in a pinball machine. As for anything one might call value or morality—that is, any standard for right or wrong—it's said to be something beyond the realm of concern for the properly scientific evolutionist.

What our work and our journal was filled with was the discretely scholarly belly-aching and cautiously scholarly hell-raising of scientists of all kinds from all around the world who were privately fed up with and appalled by the inadequacy of the mainstream theory and story. And what has happened? Such is the chill of the Glacier and the top-down control of the Domination system that only a tiny fraction of our huge body of work has even made it past the gatekeepers to reach the minds of anyone empowered to better our world.

That sentence slips by so easily that I fear the vital point can be missed.

In other words, the significance of what happened, and still happens, to the work of this increasingly large number of progressive scientists is this. Such is the power of the system bent on holding in place social, economic, political, and educational as well as religious domination that it is literally easier to fly to the moon than to effect the more basic changes in the prevailing mindset that our species needs not only to live up to its potential, but long term even to survive. Legitimized by the mindset that took over science as well as religion earlier, the prevailing paradigm for the theory and story of human evolution has succeeded in excluding almost all of this work from gaining hold in the minds of practically everybody who was anybody with a say on what is to be done or not to be done in all areas of our lives.

That's an awfully sweeping statement, yes. But it is also horribly true.

So little progress was being made in cracking the socially, economically, and politically entrenched NeoDarwinian mindset of survival of the fittest and selfishness *uber alles*—which I came to see had, among other things, given us Adolf Hitler, the Robber Barons of both the 1890s and the 1990s, and the Bushite disaster—that I was driven to add to the thrust of Riane's work, and mine with her, the direct attack on the problem in terms basically of moral evolution, which, no doubt, will close out my days.

With brilliant chapters by Riane, to this end I organized, edited, and produced two books of papers by GERGites, *The Evolutionary Outrider: The Impact of the Human Agent on Evolution* (Praeger, 1998), and *The Great Adventure: Toward a Fully Human Theory of Evolution* (SUNY Press, 2004).

To tell the story of the discovery of the lost top half for Darwin's theory, and how for a century it was shoved out of mind by the "powers-that-be," I have written and am now publishing not just one, but six books to make up for more than 100 years of suppression for "the other side of Darwin," which we'll look at in the next chapter.

SIXTEEN
MY BOOKS

Looking back on my own creative life, the image of myself that comes to mind is of an unwelcome juggler in a vaudeville show. Here was this strange figure, outdated or trying out tricks before their time, who, despite being repeatedly booed off stage, kept persisting.

Other than this embarrassing if not lunatic level of persistence, the most remarkable thing about this juggler was the incredible number and variety of balls he kept active in the air above and around him.

Occasionally he was tolerated, even once or twice getting a reasonably good hand. But then the mood set firmly against him. Down from the management came instructions that under no circumstances was he to be allowed in the theater, much less back stage.

With this juggler in mind, my books and theories sort into three stages that roughly follow the course of my life: the preparations, the accepted, and—once it was clear where I was headed—the cursed.

The preparations included all the unpublished novels, short stories, plays, and poems of my serious early private life. In my next married, parent, and bread-winner life, to this earlier pile were added probably somewhere around half a million pages of news stories, magazine articles, proposals, speeches for others, and promotional copy written for hire. This first stage of preparations concluded with the small mountain of papers, reports, and ever more escalating proposals written to become and then function as a bona fide social and systems scientist.

All of which indicates how much more writing is a matter of a 100 mile marathon—or a grinding, gasping, swimming, to cycling, to running triathalon—than the prevailing fantasy that all it involves is luck and something like a junior high school 100 yard dash.

The accepted include the books that at times against incredible indifference or opposition I managed to push uphill into publication.

My first was the award-winning *The Healing of a Nation* (Norton, 1971; Delta, 1972). Then came *The Leadership Passion: A Psychology of Ideology* (Jossey-Bass, 1977). *The Knowable Future: A Psychology of Forecasting and Prophecy* (Wiley, 1978). The widely popular *The Sphinx and the Rainbow: Brain, Mind, and Future Vision* (which blossomed from New Science Library, 1983, to Bantam New Age, 1984, out across the sea into two German, a Japanese, and a Dutch edition) and its updating in *An Arrow Through Chaos* (Inner Traditions, 2000). And the two books on evolution theory I've mentioned, with chapters by GERG members and other scholars, of which I was the originator, designer, and editor, *The Evolutionary Outrider: The Impact of the Human Agent on Evolution* (Praeger, 1998), and *The Great Adventure: Toward a Fully Human Theory of Evolution* (SUNY Press, 2004).

Hovering between the dream in manuscript and the in-print reality, however, was the cumulation that for many years shimmered before me like the chimera of a Pike's Peak rising from the desert—the books dashed out in a great quantity, which I came to think of as "the cursed."

My pattern was to write them in a great burst of enthusiasm, then on failing to find publisher interest I would set them aside and rush on to the next enthusiasm. In this way, first in box after box of manuscript and

3,000 Years of Love

then in file after file in my computer, I accumulated the blessing of a private library of the "cursed," which to me now is of the greatest fascination and challenge.

For all these books so long set aside while I rushed on are at last being published—a new one, indeed, coming out every two or three months.

Surely this must be a world record of some kind. To have *twenty*, and very likely more new books, in effect coming out all at once, by an author in his *eighties*!

How was and is this possible? Essentially it's been through that crucial experience that through the ups and downs of the roller coaster of hopes and despair over a lifetime all of us are driven to seek: the discovery of myself.

I realized that unless I stopped writing and piling them up and rushing on to another they would all die with me. In effect, I switched from writer, to editor, and then to publisher. And out of the uncanny process of my older mind, settled and now more sure of itself, discovering gold in the hurried and uncertain output of my younger self, I found what still fills me with wonderment. For in all the manuscripts piled up by that driven, sometimes wayward, often despairing, but relentlessly persistent younger self, I came to see I didn't have merely a marketable book or two. I had four *cycles* of what I'm now convinced will include some potentially lasting and meaningful books.

Time may decide this is insupportable jutzpah. On the other hand it may not. There they are. A potentially revolutionary six book Darwin Anniversary Cycle. Another potentially revolutionary six book Moral Evolution Cycle. But also—at least with the potential for a wider appeal—are the three or four books of an Entertainment and Humor

Cycle and the three or four books of a Love Cycle.

As with my "acceptable" books, here again all of this other type, which I wrote to try to befuddle, divert, slip past, or otherwise outwit the "curse," sort into a pattern of three.

Least of the triad are the books I wrote in pursuit of my adventures in the so-called other world of the paranormal. These I kept back from publication because—in a scientific world still the captive of a paradigm cocked against this vital probe of the full range of our human powers—as long as I was still building a reputation in science I couldn't afford to be identified with the heretical explorers of telepathy, precognition, remote viewing, energy healing, and the rest of it.

With Riane along for the journey, in our joint biography *3,000 Years of Love* I briefly touch on a bit of it. And in an interesting mix of detective, adventure, romance, and travel story published almost in tandem with this book, *Return to Amalfi*, I tell of the investigation of a strange and fascinating past life that may or may not have been mine 300 years ago in Italy. *The Adventures of a Sunday Psychic* and *The Further Adventures of a Sunday Psychic* may also some day be in print.

Still into the bin for the unpublished I must, for the time being, toss all my ventures into sociological community studies, the psychology of futurism, scientific methodology, and a half dozen or so other tentative ventures of this kind. Scheduled now for publication, however, are the offbeat children's stories of *Grandfather's Garden,* which I'm currently planning to illustrate. Now also at last published is the rousing story of nine generations of my mother's family of funny story tellers and fiercely independent thinkers, *Brave Laughter.* And the offbeat humor and hell-raising critique of politics and the book world *Tangled Tales of the Book Trade, or the Mystery of the Missing Centuries.*

3,000 Years of Love

It is the two peaks that for so long hovered there in and out of the mist, however, that still most haunt and drive me: the Moral Evolution cycle and the Darwin cycle.

Midway through my sixties I came to the conclusion and decision I see now as pivotal for my life. Amid the planetary signals of environmental degradation, nuclear proliferation, and a prefiguring of the potential end-game horrors of terrorism, the conclusion I reached was that without a dramatic new boost to *moral* evolution our species is doomed. I decided to devote the rest of my life to look within all the fields of science for the consensus, which I felt was there, on what might constitute the foundations of moral evolution and ways of accelerating it, or of gaining moral transformation.

Entirely on my own, with no grant or institutional support, within a few years I identified six foundations grounded in science. Another year of research revealed they were much the same for the great spiritual visionaries and progressive moral philosophers.

How exciting that was!

To find that down beneath all the surface hatred, slaughter, and seemingly eternal conflict, spanning the wide range for the varying people and cultures of this world, there was this consensus.

And going back in time, to find it spanned the thousands of years of the reign of religion, giving way to the reign of philosophy, giving way to the reign of science, which I now found *confirmed*, rather than conflicted, with the higher stream of vision for all three.

I took this scientific/philosophic/spiritual consensus and translated it into a relatively simple six point statement for the Global Ethic that the Union of Concerned Scientists as well as the World Parliament of Religions and such endearing figures as the Dalai Lama were calling for.

David Loye

Without knowing it at the time, I see now that my first three published books, *The Healing of a Nation, The Leadership Passion,* and *The Knowable Future,* were precursors for my moral evolution cycle. These earlier books still fell within the acceptable boundaries for the expression of any passion for doing good in the world. But with my first all-out, straight-talking, go-to-the-core-of-things venture in this direction came what still, after all these years, remains to me the astonishment of the systems-protective power of the paradigm of the Glacier and the Blade and the Dominator Way.

The test of tests (to me, at least) was, and is, *The River and the Star: The Lost Story of the Great Explorers of the Better World.* In keeping with what reviewers of my published books earlier praised as my gift as a science writer, *The River and the Star* brings to life the personality, mind, times, and woefully neglected morally-oriented works of the famous founders of social science and some of their most important successors—Kant, Marx and Engels, Spencer, Durkheim, Freud, Piaget, Fromm, Rokeach, Kohlberg and Gilligan.

Here is a book exploring the implications for moral transformation of the central concepts animating democracy and the most hopeful aspects of modern times—the progressive political thrust of the values of the River of equality and the Star of freedom. Could it possibly be resisted by a publisher?

Earlier during the 20th century, it would have been quickly accepted and widely read. But as the catastrophic rightward regression for America and American publishing deepened during the 1990s I became convinced there wasn't a publisher in America who would touch it.

So inspired that at times the words poured out of me almost as in a trance, I set out to give to each of the six foundations for moral transformation I had uncovered the whole book that the material for each foundation justified. First came *The Glacier and the Flame, Book I: Rediscovering Goodness.* Then *The Glacier and the Flame, Book II: Redefining Evil.* Then as I became more clearly aware of what I was up against both in terms of national regression and my own narrowing life span, bitterly and in sadness I decided to cut back the six I'd originally planned to a trilogy. Shortly now, as I write, the first two will be published, and soon I'll craft scraps written for all the rest into *The Glacier and the Flame, Book III: A Fragment of a Vision.*

In terms of the divide and conquer machinations of the domination system in Riane's terms, or the power of the Glacier in mine, the problem here is important for all of us to understand. It is that in the battle for control of the American and the global mind whoever or whatever may attempt to deal with the subject of *moral evolution*—which threatens the ageold Powers-That-Be—is automatically excluded from mainstream trade publishing to the fringe world of three specific market slots.

There is the huge insider slot for right wing religion. There is the huge outsider slot for its polar opposite, New Age spirituality. And there is the small, insular, and lackluster slot for academia. But in terms of the inbuilt systems resistance to anything that threatens progressive change these rigidly bound fringe markets have no place for anything that fails to fall into their particular slots, as does my strange new blend of moral fervor, progressive politics, and the science of an emergent, and thereby still alien, new perspective on evolution.

To get around this problem, I originally tried a tactic, which, blessed be, is now still another book to help melt the Glacier. Perhaps disguised within a small and ostensibly humorous book I might be able to sneak my core findings past the gatekeepers automatically primed to tune out on it. Perhaps a brief tale in the wry tradition of James Thurber, C.S.Lewis, J.R.Tolkien, or the *Gulliver's Travels* of the morally-oriented, long ago Dean of St.Patrick's in Dublin, Jonathan Swift might do it. So now also in print is *The Parable of the Three Villages*—a blending of Riane's work with my own that tells of the discovery of the long lost ancient civilization of the wise and good "partnership model" village of Osanto, the vicious and all-too-familiar "dominator model" village of Snarlsgrrrr, and—mirroring our own global situation as a floundering mix of the two—what happened to the hapless and rudderless village of Mystifu when the fiercesome mutant Groakers crept out of the polluted sea to threaten every home.

Thus book by book I battered away at the divide and conquer dynamics of the Glacier and the Blade that in the years leading to the Bushist disaster that like a social, economic, political, and religious juggernaut, with rigid slots for publishing, worked to cement two equations in cognitive concrete: Conservative = moral, good, right, embrace it. Liberal or progressive = immoral, bad, wrong, avoid it .

When I found the lost "top half" for Darwin's theory of evolution the GERG years led me to I thought that surely here at last was the way to crack the ice and blunt the blade. Over 100 years the idea that the evolution of *our* species, *human* evolution, chiefly depends on the ethos of the domination model—that is, the drive of "survival of the fittest" and "selfish genes"—was entrenched. Yet with nothing more than a simple computer-driven word count, I found that in the book in which Darwin tells us he is now going to look at *human* evolution, *The Descent of Man*, he wrote only *twice* of "survival of the fittest," but of *love* he wrote 95 times! Of moral sensitivity 92 times! And of the drive of brain

3,000 Years of Love

and mind 200 times!

Behind the word counts I uncovered the scientific astonishment of a long ignored completion and expansion for Darwin's theory that radically changes both the scientific and the social picture for our understanding of evolution at all levels.

Surely this was news to sufficiently open the way to publication for the rest of my works over the rest of my days. But so powerful was the money-making hold of this paradigm on the publishing world that it has left me with a story to which perhaps only Charles Dickens, with his probe of the case of Jarndyce vs. Jarndyce in *Bleak House,* or the trials of Oliver Twist or David Copperfield, could do justice.

This is the story behind the writing of *Darwin's Lost Theory* and my Darwin Anniversary Cycle, for which I found six books were required to make up for the neglect, distortion, and suppression of more than a century. *Bankrolling Evolution. Measuring Evolution. Darwin's Lost Theory. Darwin on Love. The Derailing of Evolution.* And *Telling the New Story.*

Now I must admit the juggler once hooked off the stage fairly dances with glee. For thanks to the technological revolution now turning the publishing world upside down and my founding of the Benjamin Franklin Press, as fast as all these books are printed they circle the world on the websites of all the main online book sellers in the U.S., Europe, and Asia, and into the catalogue for the world's largest book distributor, the Ingram Book Company, for book stores.

It is a time of immense satisfaction, not simply to see my own books in print. Book by book it's even more meaningful to me to see the books of others—Riane's, for example, and the work of an American successor to the great French artist and political cartoonist Honore Daumier, Bill

Bates—being published by this new progressive press.

In a terrible time it is that best of all possible worlds to see there being surely set in place this Benjamin Franklin Press to go on publishing "books to rebuild the American mind, heart, and soul" long after Riane and I are gone.

How will this story end? Will the real Darwin be welcomed back from exile? Will Kant, Freud, and all the rest get a new chance to speak? Will our species—or at least the progressive veneer of sense and decency we call humanity—make it through the 21st century?

Stay tuned. Who knows what may happen.

SEVENTEEN
OUR THEORIES

One thing I learned from the GERG experience was the difference between Europeans and Americans on the matter of theories. Americans tend to discount them as alien, impractical, or at best a questionable or insubstantial academic indulgence. Europeans, by contrast, tend to venerate theorists with the excitement and respect earlier accorded royalty.

Repeatedly I saw this in the contrast between the civic excitement of the hosts for our GERG symposia—ornate programs, special dinners, welcoming speeches by Mayors—and what awaited us on return home. We faced trade book editors fearful of "too much about theory."

Other than what was stamped with an academic requirement for anyone pretending to be educated to be able to cough up to pass a test, it was almost as if for most Americans theory didn't exist. Over years of drilling, one learned to associate the word with Einstein or Freud. But beyond that it was something neither to be trusted or bothered with.

Yet one of the things that bound Riane and me together, I see clearly now, was our mutual understanding of, and fascination with, the power of theory. Riane had originally come from a continent devastated by the theory of the Aryan Superman, with the subjugation or eradication of all "lesser" races a holy mission. Returning to finish college after the war,

David Loye

I had speedily gone from being a confused and corn-fed intellect with little more than high level Christianity holding my mind together to the worship of this incredibly exciting new thing: theory.

First my mind and being exploded with the wonder of Freud, then Marx from A to Z. Then later, when in early middle age I left the business world to go back to school, the wonders of Max Weber, Emile Durkheim, Vilfredo Pareto and the expanding ranks of all the great minds who were the founders of social science.

The power of theory, essentially, is that it makes it possible to get down beneath the confusing, multi-factor surface of things to identify a small interacting set of prime factors, and state how their interaction produces what we see and deal with as the surface end product. This getting down under and behind what happens becomes the *theory*, which becomes the crucial guide for us to what is going to happen—or to how to make it happen—instead of floundering on in helpless ignorance.

Thus, if I do say so myself, because of this interest and training I was as if by fate empowered to recognize the level of what was emerging from Riane—and this better than herself at first, able to insist on what she at first found it hard to believe.

While others at times glimpsed the potential importance of her work as a theorist, for some years I felt that only the great anthropologist Ashley Montagu and I fully and sufficiently recognized her real emerging stature.

Then at last it came—a high point for my life as well as hers. Macrohistory is the study of theories about the patterns that have shaped social policy, action, and recorded history over long spans of time. With several centuries to draw from, in *Macrohistory and Macrohistorians* two male scholars of international status selected and wrote of the twenty macrohistorians they had decided were the most important.

As was to be expected, it was, in essence, the Good Old Boys Club of Great Thinkers. First came the unfamiliar, except to specialists: Ssu-Ma Ch'ien, Augustine, Khaldun, Vico. Then came the better known: Adam Smith, Hegel, Comte, Marx, Spencer, Pareto, Weber, Steiner, Spengler, Teilhard de Chardin, Sorokin, Toynbee, Gramsci, Sarker—and Riane Eisler.

The first woman, as well as the only living person, to become a member of the Good Old Boy's Club of the otherwise safely dead.

Throughout her books runs the interplay of the findings and stories of many fields and a wide range of theories and works by others to ground the case for her own theories, perspective, and convictions. Chaos theory, biological and cultural evolution theories, theories of the patterning for prehistory and history, the findings of archeology, anthropology, psychology, sociology, systems science, the rich new 20th century source of gender studies and feminist scholarship—it is a heady mix her light touch keeps afloat and the reader engaged.

Out of this mix rise the pillars of her *cultural transformation theory* and the study of *relational dynamics*. The grounding for both is in the radically differing configurations for the *domination model* and the *partnership model* of personal and social organization and governance.

Two earlier alternative names for the pair begin to get across the differences as they are specific to gender. The domination or *androcratic model* (deriving from the Greek "andros" for man) prevails wherever the male and everything stereotypically labeled masculine is accorded the highest value, with female and the stereotypically feminine ranked as distinctly lower. The partnership or *gylanic model* (a made-up word from the Greek *gyne* for woman and *andros* for man) is of an equality of the sexes or genders, with neither masculine nor feminine valued over the other.

Across the span of human evolution, in groups of every type, Riane shows how three radically contrasting components set off these two basic guidance models from one another. The domination model not only values male over female but ranks all other differences into superior and inferior. It is held in place and advanced with the threat and brutal backup of violence of all kinds. It is locked in place with the top-down control of tyranny and authoritarian governance in *both* the family and the state or tribe.

By contrast, the partnership model values equality of gender and other differences. It is advanced by peaceful means rather than violence. It is locked in place with free inquiry and other qualities of democracy, and it supports relations of mutuality, of linking and bonding.

An important observation—and aspect of her theory—contradicts the customary assumption that the partnership model must mean a matter of unquestioning cooperation, and consensus, with nobody more important than anybody else, or no "hierarchies." As Riane brings out again and again, there are hierarchies in the partnership model. But rather than *hierarchies of domination,* backed up by fear and force, there are what she calls *hierarchies of actualization.* Here respect, accountability, and benefit don't just flow from the bottom up (as in the domination model) but both ways. And leadership and power are also different. Rather than being defined as the power to dominate and destroy (to give orders that must be unquestioningly obeyed), power is empowering rather than disempowering: the more stereotypically feminine power to give and nurture life symbolized by the Chalice rather than the Blade.

3,000 Years of Love

For most of recorded history, as her work documents with precision, the domination model has ruled the roost. The partnership model prevailed in the early Neolithic cradles of civilization and more technologically advanced later civilizations such as Minoan Crete and the Indus valley cultures of India. Cultures orienting to the partnership model can still be found in tribal cultures such as the Muso of China described by Chinese scholars in *The Chalice and The Blade in Chinese Culture* and the Minangkabau of Sumatra, studied by University of Pennsylvania anthropologist Peggy Sanday. This configuration can also be seen today in the Nordic nations, which regularly rank high in the United Nations Human Development Reports on quality of life.

Perhaps of greatest importance in the long range, or macrohistorical, perspective are the patterns she substantiates for her theory of cultural transformation. In the early civilizations there was a long period of a predominantly partnership or gylanic culture. Then came the radical shift to a predominantly dominator or androcratic culture roughly 5,000 years ago, followed by periodic attempts for partnership resurgence. Then about 300 years ago began a shift back in the partnership direction—today posing a critical challenge and critical choice.

But counterposed to every gain in a progressive partnership direction has been the build up of a fierce regressive backlash—such as we are struggling to free ourselves of once again today.

Counter-revolution versus revolution, de-volution versus evolution—for every progressive step forward comes the regressive attempt to shove us one or two steps backward.

And so within what to most people seems no more than a matter of partisan politics in fact lies the struggle for human evolution versus a return to the old, "pure" dominator reign of the few over the many. In terms of the environmental and all the other global threats mounting against us today, what is at stake is the ultimate choice of planetary life or death.

This is just my sketch of the richness—and global implications—of Riane's cultural transformation theory. Here, for the flavor of her own thoughts and language, is the passage through which she started to introduce it in her 1987 book *The Chalice and the Blade.*

"Socialists and communists assert that the root of our problems is capitalism; capitalists insist socialism and communism are leading us to ruin. Some argue our troubles are due to our 'industrial paradigm,' that our 'scientific worldview' is to blame. Still others blame humanism, feminism, and even secularism, pressing for a return to the 'good old days' of a smaller, simpler, more religious age.

"Yet, if we look at ourselves—as we are forced to by television or the grim daily ritual of the newspaper at breakfast—we see how capitalist, socialist, and communist nations alike are enmeshed in the arms race and all the other irrationalities that threaten both us and our environment. And if we look at our past—at the routine massacres by Huns, Romans, Vikings, and Assyrians, or the cruel slaughters of the Christian Crusades and Inquisition—we see there was even more violence and injustice in the smaller, prescientific, preindustrial societies that came before us."

"Weaving together evidence from art, archaeology, religion, social science, history, and many other fields of inquiry into new patterns that more accurately fit the best available data, *The Chalice and the Blade* tells a new story of our cultural origins. It shows that war and the 'war of the sexes' are neither divinely nor biologically ordained. And it provides verification that a better future is possible—and is in fact firmly rooted in the haunting drama of what actually happened in our past."

My Theories

Riane's theories, as we've seen, are grounded in the historic tension between the Domination way of life symbolized by the Blade in contrast to the Partnership way of life symbolized by the Chalice. For me a central grounding has been the counterpart image of the freezing of heart and mind and soul by the Glacier of control (conformity, moral insensitivity, regression) that repeatedly tries to snuff out the Flame of freedom (creativity, moral sensitivity, progression).

Here is how I put it in opening *The Glacier and the Flame I: Rediscovering Goodness.*

"You work for civil rights, the women's movement, the environment, peace, an end to poverty or homelessness—on and on the causes rise. And then as inevitable as the ending of day with night, something like the chill wind blown off an immense glacier reaches into our lives to snuff out the flame of the drive of the good within us. Isn't this what happens over and over again? . . .

"We call it backlash, regression, devolution, a heinous outbreak of barbarism. But add it all up century after century and one can begin to see how tame these words, and even the most shocking of events, are for the immensity of what keeps happening to our species over and over again.

"What is this vast chill that at times with an astonishing speed, almost overnight, defying everything we have come to think of as intelligence and purpose and values, moves into our nations, cities, homes, hearts, minds, and souls to seize and numb us?

"What, in a word, is the Glacier? Where did it come from? How did it gain its power and how may we end its power?

"But also—of even greater urgency for us now to understand—what is the Flame?

"What is this quality, force, thrust, or champion of *the good* within us that no matter how often its flare is blown out, refuses to be quenched?"

From this one can glimpse the primarily moral thrust of my own body of theory, which I see now both complements and differs from Riane's in this way. Hers, as was recognized in *Macrohistory and Macrohistorians,* is a large, cohesive theory designed to embrace much going on in our heads or times, or *macro*theory. Mine, by contrast, with possibly two exceptions, are of components of the larger picture, or *micro*theories.

I first began to find them bubbling up out of me in my graduate studies in early middle age. Once securely armed with the membership card of my Ph.D., I began to develop them with each expansion into new territory for the hunger and delight of my liberated mind.

The interest in the battle of Left, Right, and Middle, and how specifically this drove us either ahead or backward politically, first engaged me. *The Healing of a Nation, The Leadership Passion, The Knowable Future*, and many scholarly papers recorded the microtheories that emerged from this exploration.

Of them the most interesting aspect to me in retrospect is to see how I was driven not just to state what I saw and let it go at that. The most delightful aspect of these ventures to me was the use of interviews and formal experiments, surveys, and the rest of the fascinating methodologies of science to develop a series of measures to test my insights to prove them right or wrong.

In this way I developed the Ideological Matrix Profile, or IMP for short, to both express and test my theories of Right, Left, Middle dynamics. Sure enough, as I speculated, they confirmed that we progress or regress politically according to whether conservatives or liberals push us to the tipping point for the M-Shift—or the shift by the semi-fluid mass of us in the middle to Right or to Left.

Next came Hemispheric Consensus Prediction, or the HCP, to test my theories of the dynamics of left brain, right brain, and frontal brain interaction in the prediction of the future. In *The Knowable Future* and the still unpublished *Making It in the Dream Factory*—in which use of the HCP foretold the phenomenal success of the Star Wars movie cycle even before release of the first movie—I record the startling degree to which consensus, or the guess in common, for right brain and left brain dominant people predicts the future. This versus the guess of right brain dominant "psychics" or left brain dominant "economists" alone—to which we are still chiefly locked in at all levels of our life and economy.

The results for PSP confirmed my hunch that right brain dominant people had a secret way that might at times allow them to successfully leap ahead in mind into the future, in contrast to the left brain dominant who remained flat-footed not only in the present but in the past. But PSP was the acronym for *Psychic* Sensitivity Profile. As this was then, and still largely remains, forbidden territory for science this work still languishes in old notes somewhere.

Then came the venture that provided the stepping stone, or neglected alleyway, into what I hope to be remembered for some day. I realize today that MSP was to some extent, to quote that haunting passage from Thomas Wolfe's *Look Homeward, Angel,* "a stone, a leaf, an unfound door . . ."

MSP stood for Moral Sensitivity Profile. Thinking of this measure now, I feel that regret that once in a while must come to all of us. That memory of the passing in and out of one's life of someone or something exceptionally engaging, exceptionally meaningful at the time. And the sense now of great unrealized possibilities.

On the surface MSP was nothing more than a brief questionnaire with a string of names of wellknown historical or current figures or celebrities and the request, "Please check those who are either most meaningful or most interest you."

Buried within the string of names was the fact that all were either identified with moral action or sensitivity—for example, Martin Luther King, Jr., anti-nuclear activist Helen Caldecott; or were morally "neutral"—baseball icon Joe Dimaggio, some popular singers and movie stars.

By correlating results with other measures I found that this simple instrument seemed to not only accurately identify the morally sensitive but also predict prosocial behavior.

A seemingly minor result, I know, but the venture foreshadowed what over the years ahead became my development of moral transformation theory, evolutionary action theory, a triadic theory of—and new language for—evolution, and my reconstruction and promotion of a liberating new update, expansion, and understanding of Darwinian theory.

Merely to set it down this way makes me want to shut up now and close. It sounds so immodest, so boastful, so over-blown—and indeed so unlikely.

Out of the long ago, prolonged childhood undermining of

confidence in my mind and myself as anything out of ordinary, which I've struggled all my life to break free of, the long ago old me comes back to say, "Hey, wait a minute there. Are you sure? Could all this really have come out of you? Better play it safe and make a joke of it. Or just not play it up so much. For the world waits with a snub, or cutting remark, or foot to tromp on ostensibly big thinking. Better play it safe and quit while you're ahead."

But from the beginning there has been in me, as in Riane, as in scores of people whose friendship I've cherished over the years this something that refuses to be put down, that persists.

As the great firebrand poet William Blake put it, "If the Sun and Moon should Doubt, they'd immediately go out."

Out of the books now at last gaining print, briefly and quickly now, I will set down here what the four bodies of work and theories I've identified amount to.

Seizing me in the late 1980s, moral transformation theory grew out of the experience and project I've already described. I had this hunch that within the great sprawl of both natural and social science one could find the firm foundations for what is right and what is wrong. Here are the six in the form of "The Code of Osanto," into which I put them in *The Parable of the Three Villages*, which I wrote for easy popular reading.

Foundation one: For guidance, let us listen to the inbuilt voice of goodness rather than the imposed voices of brutality within ourselves.

Foundation two: Relating as human to human and to the whole of nature and the cosmos, let us embrace the partnership way of life and reject the dominator way of life.

Foundation three: Act—and let this be our standard for judging the actions of ourselves and others: to advance *both* freedom and equality, never the one without the other.

Foundation four: Let us seek and open our hearts to the power of love.

Foundation five: Let us seek and open our minds to the power of the Guidance System of Higher Mind.

Foundation six: May we be the torch that not only lights up the darkness but also shows and leads the way to the better future—or, more simply put, let us be and do good in the world.

Evolutionary Action Theory—as I've described it in *The Evolutionary Outrider: The Impact of the Human Agent on Evolution* (Praeger, 1998)—"shows how the active human agent can much more rapidly advance our evolution at a critical point of challenge. It outlines a new evolutionary action theory based on Darwin's long-ignored theory of the moral sense, and Eisler's and others' works in psychology, brain research, and a wide range of other fields."

Beyond that it covers too much to attempt to summarize here, but on re-reading it does seem to me a well-constructed statement of exactly what it purports to be and do.

A Triadic Theory and New Language for Evolution has for some time now only existed in a talk I gave with slides at an annual meeting of the American Cybernetic Society. But now I plan to use it as the opening section for a new book length completion of my past-published scientific papers, to be titled *a Triadic Theory, New Language for Evolution, and Other Heresies.*

Again I can do no more than note that this triadic theory is based on my discovery of an underlying consensus, among current and earlier great scientists and philosophers, on a three factor theory of evolution going clear back to the flamboyant early Greek philosopher Empedocles. Along with this, in a series of hand-drawn cartoons and other visuals, I make the case for the use of a new visual language for easily tracking and explaining evolution in terms of the concepts of this triadic theory.

And so we come again to Darwin.

Again I can do no more than say it's all there in the six books of the Darwin Anniversary Cycle earlier described, along with my hope for the Global Sounding.

Out of all the research and experience of my life—in keeping with my old need to develop new measures to test new theories, and put them to effective use—this is the new measure of global health and wellbeing I've developed. Described in *Bankrolling Evolution* and *Measuring Evolution,* The Global Sounding measures the degree to which specific projects or policies are likely to advance, or check in place, or drive us backward in evolution.

In terms of the planetary requirement for sustaining and advancing life on this earth, the implications, as with Riane's work, pose the choice for us of whether we are to fulfill our great potential or annihilate ourselves.

EIGHTEEN
THE PARTNERSHIP ADVENTURE

Starting far back in our history, a major force driving the cultural evolution of our species has been the eruption of social movements.

The big movements are well known—the spiritual advances that followed the emergence of Jesus, Gautama, Lao-Tsu, and others, which followers shaped to either progressive or regressive ends in this Earth's major religions. The amorphous freedom movement that sparked and drove the American, French, and ill-fated Russian revolutions. Well known in their time were hundreds of the smaller social movements that for a while focus on some problem or issue and then fade as their immediate purpose is realized, or—at least for the time being—they're crushed or stifled. Thus, millions of people in the closing years of the 20th century rallied to the call of the civil rights, peace, environmental, human potentials, women's, and "healthy living" movements.

The pattern in common to these movements is that usually a charismatic figure or charismatic book forcefully expresses a widely felt need. In terms of chaos theory, this thrust of the Flame becomes the "strange" or chaotic attractor to which thousands of people are drawn as to the vortex in a whirlpool of potential change impacting society.

This happened with publication of *The Chalice and the Blade.* What sprang up was a Partnership Movement animated by the feeling that in

3,000 Years of Love

this book Riane had come up with the best answer yet to the age-old question of "deep down, what is wrong with our world and what can we do about it?"

Like all other movements, ours was distinguished by enormous hopes, occasional great peaks of accomplishment and satisfaction, but also more irritations, worries, and disappointments than we could ever have imagined in setting out.

"Drop it!" we were often advised by those who had similarly written charismatic books and then found themselves saddled with a social movement, such as our good friend Hazel Henderson, ex-founder and for a time slave to the Princeton Center for Alternative Futures. But following our co-founding of the Center for Partnership Studies in 1988, over the years hundreds of remarkably fine and wonderful people whose lives became intertwined with ours kept the Center and the Partnership Movement going. At its best, it bound us together in a sense of the grand adventure and the good fight that took us to the exotic as well as all the down-home meaningful places for this movement.

An early high point for the partnership movement came in 1992 when 500 people from fifty countries streamed to the island of Crete for the First International Partnership Conference.

As I wrote of earlier, a place and time of greatest meaning and charisma for our understanding of the earlier partnership culture is the civilization of Minoan Crete, which pre-dated and then overlapped with the early Egyptian dynasties.

As we are in such informational overload these days, with minds that quickly erase whatever we've just read or heard in order to have room for whatever's next, I think a few points will bear repeating. As I've indicated, it was a culture like no other of its time and few since then in combining a high order of arts and crafts with the precursor of practically everything we have come to think of as the best aspects of civilization. An orientation toward peace rather than war. Good roads. Well-planned towns and cities. Housing notable for its beauty and practicality. A knack for trade in agricultural products and artifacts, via a great maritime fleet throughout the Mediterranean, which provided Minoan Crete with the kind of economy in which seemingly everybody shared. There is no evidence of poverty here, either in actuality or by inference. At the other end of the scale, there's also no evidence of any huge disparities in wealth, for the vast gap between the rich and the poor that remains the great affliction of our species is absent there.

There is also no evidence of the mighty ruler or ruling elites who despotically beat and bashed both people and a self-promotional history into shape. The only artifactual evidence of anyone in a leadership role is that of the "Procession Fresco" showing a woman who appears to be a high priestess, with arms raised in benediction, receiving offerings from groups of priestesses and priests. Nor are these "rulers" memorialized with immense and intimidating statues, while the "subjects" are tiny figures cowering below them, as was already common then in Egypt and remained so in much of history. Both priestess and those bearing gifts to her are of the same size, on the same level. This remarkable equality is further indicated by the size of the only thing they have found that appears to be a "throne"—a small, delicately crafted wooden chair in one chamber in the "palace" at Knossos that could, at best, have held no more than 50 people.

The archeological research of Sir Arthur Evans and the great 20th century archeologists Nicolas Platon and Maria Gimbutas—both of whom we came to know, Gimbutas particularly well—reveals all this.

3,000 Years of Love

Along with Riane's monumental systems analysis placing this culture within the sweep of 35,000 years of human evolution, what can still today be seen with one's own eyes reveals that in the ruins and artifacts of Minoan Crete we have compelling evidence of what can flower on this earth from a greater sharing of power in all areas of life on the basis of a reasonably effective degree of mutually respectful equality.

Riane's analysis shows that the combination of peace, a high degree of creativity, and the healthy economy with the assurance of benefits for all, which went along with a power-balanced relationship of women and men, was no coincidence.

Haunting to think of it now, looking back from the perspective of an earth ravaged and devastated now for 5,000 years by dominator systems, it was the pent-up yearning for some way of re-enacting and reclaiming this ethos that pulled 500 people from 50 nations to Crete for the conference.

It was the way Riane evoked all this in *The Chalice and the Blade* that originally caught up the imagination of the First Lady of Greece, Margarita Papandreou, wife of Greek Premier Andreas Papandreou. She wrote Riane of her enthusiasm for the book, and out of their relationships emerged the vision that an international partnership conference might be staged there in Crete. As I wrote of earlier, we flew to Greece to confer with Margarita and her aides. Soon the idea was taking shape in the form of an event that would combine both intellectual content—that is, talks by Riane and other scholars about the unique wonder of the ancient Minoan civilization and its implications for our troubled time—and the Minoan art in all its forms.

There would be a graphic arts festival. There would be dancing in both ancient and modern forms. There would be music ranging from

Greek folk to classic quartets. There was even a good chance that the ancient sport of bull-leaping, which as noted is so dramatically portrayed in one of the most famous Minoan murals, could be revived for display.

A particularly intriguing feature would be the premiere performance of what proved to be the haunting score for a piece written by one of modern Greece's greatest composers, whose name I have unfortunately forgotten. This would accompany a chorus and dancers performing what seemed to those soaked in the ancient culture to have likely been the prevailing form of ritual dance. There would also be tours of the beautiful, crumbling, multi-leveled grandeur of the "palace" at Knossos, as well as visits to other sites of the early Minoan culture elsewhere on the island.

Margarita Papandreou was a fascinating figure. Tall, lanky, still strikingly beautiful in her mid-sixties, she was an American by birth, from somewhere in the midwest, as I recall. She had met Andreas Papandreou when they were both students at the University of Chicago. Returning to Greece with him, she had become an invaluable partner in his rise in political life, gaining a cult status among women of Greece and elsewhere comparable to the fervor once felt for Jackie Kennedy or Eleanor Roosevelt in the U.S.

We met with her and her aides first at a sumptuous buffet supper on the verandah of a villa she had in one of the seaport towns. There was a basketball court nearby, and at one point during the evening Margarita—clad in frilly and elegant evening attire with high heels—grabbed up a basketball and dribbled it over the court for a leap to deftly sink a basket. Grinning, she explained she had been a championship basketball player in her high school days back in the U.S.

Given this opening for another touch of Americana and the rustic,

I playfully mentioned I was from Oklahoma and a good harmonica player. As this intrigued her and the Greek delegation, I hauled out my trusty Hohner Blues Harp and played a few bars of "Moon River" and "Jimmy Crack Corn" to cement our cross-cultural relationships.

And so it came to be as planned—a spectacular event and experience for all concerned. People streamed in from around the world, with hundreds turned back as the number was restricted to only 500 by the limit for the housing available for the event. Some tensions did develop—a group of Margarita's Marxist devotees tried to force a favorable vote on a pro-Palestinian resolution condemning Israel. In terms of group dynamics, it seemed to me this was also an attempt to pit Margarita against Riane, as if with more than a touch of antisemitism, and in keeping with the fierce abiding requirement for the dominator model, their champion must outshine the Jewish contender for top dog status in the gathering. But by and large it was a big lovefest for all involved, with bonds formed among many of those who first met there that still last to this day.

Particularly memorable was the attempt to launch a partnership youth movement under the leadership of young Robin Krieglstein. I remember how his father, Chicago professor Werner Krieglstein and his wife Mary Ann, stood up during an open, full chamber discussion to tell the assembly of how they had been influenced by Riane's book in their building of a partnership family valuing cross-generational as well as gender equality. Then up stepped this slender young man, hardly bearded as yet. Alongside him was a fervent knot of young women and other young men.

A special stillness settled within that gathering of older, battle-scarred and doubtful yet still hopeful, peaceful warriors for the better life. In a clear and confident voice young Robin told of the behind-scenes discussions of his friends and how they planned to carry forth the dream worldwide among those of their generation in all the countries represented there.

Looking upon those bright eyes and eager faces, with all their lives before them, hearing this young voice of confident leadership ring out, there was, I'm sure, for most of us there that day the thrill of a sense of some reassurance that, with time and the passing of the torch from the older to younger oncoming generations, the dream might some day come to be.

The most exciting phase for the partnership adventure was the rapid spread of "partnership education centers" across the U.S. and into Europe and Asia. A telephone call or letter from an enthusiastic reader of Riane's book would come in. What could they do to help accelerate the shift from a dominator to a partnership world?

I came to see the most important thing for us to do was not to just tell them to send money to the Center, or write a letter to an editor. It was to encourage and empower them to forge ahead on their own.

Here were all these people accustomed to holding up their hands in school to ask permission to go to the bathroom. Or later on, accustomed to come up with ideas practically all of which had to be passed on for enactment or endorsed by higher authority. So they had become accustomed to the idea encouraged and perpetuated by the dominator system that nothing could be done without permission or money from higher up, and so tamely accepted the fact that most of their ideas went nowhere.

This was just the way the world was, be grateful you had a chance to speak and settle back to forget it—and so the world inched forward where maybe otherwise it could have leaped.

We suggested they simply get together with other local enthusiasts for the book, declare themselves a Center for Partnership Education, and on their own develop workshops and everything else needed to enlist the energies and enthusiasms of like-minded, potential partnership folk. I developed and talked up the mantra "self-organizing, self-directing, and self-financing."

What happened then put us in touch with a rapidly widening circle of wonderful people with a knack for the kind of creative leadership generally discouraged, boxed-in, or stifled with the dominator model constraints still largely prevailing in America and globally.

Del Jones, a fiery Arizonian, became an early key figure in the movement, organizing annual partnership conferences in the United States and founding the Partnership Education Center in Tucson that still flourishes today. Dagmar, the crusading wife of a former governor of Ohio, Dick Celeste, started a center in Columbus, Ohio. A bright, black woman from Liberia, Mignonette Pellegrin, who had migrated to Hawaii and become a successful businesswoman, opened an active center in Oahu. Professor Krieglstein and an old time hell-for-leather activist, Jane Heckman, with a dedicated core of others launched a particularly active Center in Chicago after *The Chicago Tribune* published a special section on Riane's book and vision. Other centers sprang up in New York, North Carolina, Texas, Oregon, several in California, and eventually as far away as Greece, Germany, and with publication of the book in Russia, in Moscow.

Particularly meaningful was the formation of one of these self-organizing, self-governing, and self-financing centers in the Seychelle Islands off the western coast of Africa. The key mover was an attractive, high spirited woman who was the environmental officer for the government of the islands. Putting together a group including a British attorney and constitutional law expert and native Seychelle islanders—including her own African maid as well as several other whites—out of their discussions she produced the world's first formal constitution for the goals and governance of a partnership society.

Alongside the formation of these centers emerged encouraging signs of the spread of the partnership vision within the arts. A partnership rock opera of the "Jesus Christ Superstar" variety was written and performed by a group in Michigan. More recently, a rock band emerged in Paris with Gylania for its name. Painters and sculptors were generating and exhibiting paintings and sculptures inspired by Riane's work.

Especially haunting and I believe lasting were and are the paintings of the artist Barbara Schaefer, whose evocative works of love for Riane and the partnership vision add their arresting touch to the walls of our home. The cover for this book comes from the cherished little book of paintings she gave us, each a tiny masterpiece with a rare feeling for the power of color and design.

I can still see, feel, and hear the multimedia extravaganza to benefit CPS staged in San Francisco by the gifted writer and ritualist Vicki Noble at the Galleria, a large facility with a multilevel stage normally used by leading rock groups on tour. Promoted with a lavish poster and other publicity, as Fats Waller would have put it, "the joint was jumping" with singers, story tellers, musicians and artists of Black, Native-American, and Oriental as well as White backgrounds, of both sexes, ranging in age from bopping teenagers to swinging oldsters.

Back to mind now comes a flamboyant, wise-cracking trio of young women playing the guitar, flute, and the long booming Australian aboriginal digeridoo—and one of the best pictures ever taken of Riane and me by the gorgeous Academy-award-winning film-maker and activist Vivienne Verdon-Roe.

Now also books written by others inspired by or including sections on Riane's work and the partnership vision began to appear. Using the partnership versus dominator model to go to the heart of the matter, new books probed the core dynamics for an astounding range of areas—psychology, sociology, business, government, history, religion, spirituality, as well as gender relations, child raising, and across the board for art.

The partnership vision was used by the authors of the best-seller *Megatrends*, business futurists John Naisbitt and Patricia Aburdene, to structure their later best-seller *Megatrends for Women*. Then Vice president Al Gore referred to *Chalice* in his best-seller on the environment *Earth in the Balance*. The leading Sumerian scholar Samuel Noah Kramer restructured the past in terms of the dominator-partnership model interaction in *The Myths of Enki: The Crafty God*.

On and on it went: The gripping medieval tale *High Kamilan* by Canadian writer Marie Jakober. John Robbins' *Reclaiming Our Health*. Barry and Janae Weinhold's *Breaking Free of the Co-Dependency Trap*. Linda Lindsley's *Gender Roles*. Michael Sky's *Sexual Peace*. Brian Griffith's *The Garden of Our Dreams*. Marc Allen's *The Ten Percent Solution*. David Korten's epic *The Great Turning*.

Also, as a replay for our earlier collaboration on *The Equal Rights Handbook*, was our book *The Partnership Way*, widely put to use in churches throughout the country as well as all the partnership centers,. Written by Riane and me with contributions by others in the movement—including a wonderful set of pen and ink drawings by

Carmel artists John Mason, John Thompson, Jim Beeman, and Jeff Helwig contrasting Minoan and other partnership culture art and artifacts with the later dominator era brutality of battles to the death and witch burnings—this was a handbook on how to put the new perspective into social, economic, political, educational, media, and spiritual action for the Centers and other interested parties.

From Power to Partnership was the brain child of our "surrogate son" Alfonso "Monty" Montuori. Jazz musician, systems scientist, Dean of Graduate Studies and a pioneering partnership educator at the California Institute of Integral Studies, Monty and his co-author Isabella Conti journeyed around the country to probe for the intimate details of how famous and not-so-famous people were putting the partnership approach into action in their own everyday and working lives.

All this was capped by the saga of *The Chalice and the Blade in Chinese Culture.* After *Chalice* was published in Chinese, out of the blue, from GERG's Chinese member, professor Min Jiayin, came a request for funds to launch a Partnership Research Group at the Chinese Academy for the Social Sciences in Beijing.

It was immediately obvious this was an opportunity of considerable potential. *The Chalice and the Blade* was based on Western sources. Was the pattern universal that Riane uncovered for the shift from an earlier more peaceful Goddess-oriented partnership culture to a violent male God-oriented dominator culture? Or had the pattern been different for Asia?

Riding on the answer was a matter of considerable political significance, as well as potential consequences for peace. At the core the partnership model is not only what Darwin was writing about in the suppressed completing half for his theory. It is the underlying thrust to the ethos and rationale for democracy. By aiding the formation in China of such a prestigious research group within what was still very much a post-Maoist dictatorship, could we fly in under the anti-democracy radar of the rigid communist leadership? Could we help build and strengthen a faction among influential Chinese intellectuals interested in using the seemingly harmless word "partnership"—easy to justify as obviously consonant with communism—to help push the country toward democracy and freedom?

There was no telling what good might come of it. With its huge influence on the direction into the future for all the rest of Asia, if China could even in the slightest way be nudged toward democracy here could be a lever for the change.

I used this enticement in a grant proposal to philanthropist Robert Graham, whose book *50 50 at 50* was the first to be published by the Benjamin Franklin Press. We raised $10,000, which could go a long way back then in China. Three years later, with Professor Min Jiayin as editor, in a neck to neck race with time, *The Chalice and the Blade in Chinese Culture* was finished and published both in English and Chinese in time for the United Nations Decade for Women Conference in Beijing in 1995.

The book confirmed what Riane had observed in Western prehistory. This independent group of seventeen Chinese archeologists, anthropologists, and other social scientists, with fourteen advisors, found the same pattern she had uncovered for the West also prevailed in ancient China and almost certainly was much the same for all of Asia.

As Riane wrote in her foreword to the book: "Perhaps most important, it highlights that the way gender relations are structured in both the so-called private and public spheres plays a key role in matters vital for our future: whether a society is more peaceful or warlike, more creative or destructive, more egalitarian or exploitative."

Did our little $10,000 nudge help support pro-democracy aspirations in China? There is of course no way of knowing. But popularized by chaos theory is the idea of the so-called Butterfly Effect, where hypothetically the stamping of a single butterfly in Asia—or vice versa, in America—might through systems dynamics help bring on whole systems change.

The probability is infinitesimal. But I would like to think it did.

NINETEEN
GERMANY, REGRESSION, AND THE
PUSH TO A BETTER WORLD

"Am I speaking to Riane Eisler, author of *The Chalice and The Blade*?"

The voice was pleasant, mellow, with a German accent. Increasingly delighted with the sophistication of the questions her caller was asking about the history of dominator-partnership relations and the current progress of the partnership movement in the U.S., Riane chatted with the man for a time. He had identified himself as Daniel Goudevert of the Volkswagen company in Germany.

"What do you do there?" she finally asked. "I mean, what is your job?"

There was a pause.

"I'm the Chairman of the Board," came the reply, Goudevert no doubt relishing his quiet underplaying of his prominence.

Thus began another meaningful chapter for the partnership movement. Goudevert was in fact the chairman of the giant German car manufacturer worldwide. He was enthusiastic about *The Chalice and The Blade*, having read it in the hard cover German edition published by Bertlesmann as well as in the original English edition. Within two years, he was to write the foreword to its new edition, *Kelch und Schwert* published in paperback by Goldmann Verlag.

He was an unusual man for the head of a major car manufacturer or any other company, having earlier been a professor at the Sorbonne in Paris. When later we came to meet him, he proved to be a large, handsome, affable man with light curly hair who looked a bit like former U.S. President Bill Clinton, with the same kind of energy and charm.

It turned out that prior to reading the book he himself had launched a public service venture for Volkswagen called The International Partnership Initiative. Serendipitously, the avowed purpose for IPI was to transcend the normal competitive barriers between companies and the walls of bureaucracy in governments to bring together business and government, along with the workers and intellectuals, to solve problems in targeted areas of regional and global need. The current goal for the Institute was to wash up and heal the wounds left over in East Germany by the collapse of the Communist regime.

The underlying public relations purpose was, of course—as was and is the case in all such ventures launched by private industry—to enhance the prestige of Volkswagen at top levels of government, as well as in relationships with other industries, both in Germany and Europe and elsewhere throughout the world. This in no way diminished the stature of the project, for Goudevert was not only a creative businessman, but a visionary captivated by the ethos that he had now found adequately expressed, and documented with scholarship, in Riane's work.

To further possibilities for a relation between Riane, our Center for Partnership Studies, and the International Partnership Institute, he sent his chief intellectual aide and chairman of the International Partnership Initiative to meet with and get acquainted with us over several days in Carmel.

3,000 Years of Love

Thus began the adventure of our wonderful times with the remarkable Peter Meyer-Dohm. Peter was a stately, portly, middle-aged man of many smiles yet firmly assertive, with the deep guttural German voice of the academic used to being believed without question. This he had been prior to joining Volkswagen as Goudevert's intellectual aide-de-camp. A professor of economics originally, he had been the President of Bochum University in Germany. This was the portentous guise via which we first got to know him as over several days he queried us extensively about everything about the partnership vision and movement intellectually and practically, and imparted the August goals for Goudevert's and his International Partnership Initiative. Gradually, however, our laughing, and merriment over stories and observations and interests and values we found in common lulled him into that feeling of security within which you feel you can drop the mask. Convinced now he could safely open up, he began to reveal the many other fascinating people that Peter in actuality was.

The initial persona was the one we first met—Herr Doktor Professor Peter Meyer-Dohm, the frowning intellect with the deep, rapid fire, booming voice that could quickly dominate conversation or discussion whenever he wished.

Another persona, however, which began to reveal itself in that first visit, was an elfin creature given to droll expressions and gestures. His voice jumping from the academic basement to the attic and turning from the clang of iron to playful velvet, he loved to poke fun wherever he might slyly detect that fun needed to be poked. Then as we came to know him still better though our ensuing visits to Germany, where we also came to know his lovely wife Uta, whom he adored as she adored him, there emerged his most surprising and endearing side.

David Loye

The entry point was his childlike delight in simple things, which he loved to remark—the way some gadget worked, the exquisite taste of a piece of toast, the way a new pin he had given Uta looked on her. Soon he revealed the radically different other side to life for himself and Uta and their children Johannes, Sita, and Veronika.

Known in Germany and in business and intellectual circles there as the affable but intimidating intellectual gun-slinger for Volkswagen, in radical contrast he was known among a handful of friends there and in India, where he managed to spend a good bit of time each year, as the devotee of the anti-guru Dadaji. Shedding his formal Western business attire for the proper robes and sandals worn by all the rest, Peter would sit close by the great figure he adored as the most perfect and fascinating of living beings, of whom he was to write a beautiful biography *The Fragrance of the Heart.*

I tried to capture a sense of this fascinating relationship in a poem called, simply, *Peter and Dadaji.*

Peter and Dadaji
The lyre resonates to the Presence.
All its strings are in motion, the
chords are like flights of birds
skimming the water, skimming the
treetops, seeking the high of sky.
It is in rapture over the Presence.
It fairly melts before one's eyes,
the wood becoming liquid, the
strings an ecstatic stream.

(continued)

> Stop! For it will dissolve if
> this goes on! It is too much
> for anything of this earth.
> But yet it plays on and on and
> on, delirious with the visit of
> the Presence here, there, and
> everywhere. But now what is this?
> The Lyre has become the Presence
> and the Presence the Lyre.

As at the drop of a hat Peter would tell it, Dadaji's life story was amazing. Originally he was known as the Bing Crosby of India, a crooner of popular songs. This career he abandoned to become a prosperous banker. Then one day came the experience whereby the ex-crooner and now sober banker known as Amiya Roy Chowdhury became convinced he had become, while still living, a reincarnation of a famous earlier holy man Sri Ram Thakur.

Via this inexplicable transformative experience in mid-life he became Dadaji, a holy man soon commanding a wide following because of the appeal of his message, his tolerance and droll sense of humor, and his supposed ability to perform miracles—several of which Peter reported in his book.

"All is love," Dadaji would stress over and over again. The characteristic quote with which Peter opens his book *Fragrance of the Heart* is this:

"We have come here to make love to Him, to be bathed in His Love and to vibrate His Love through the actions that come our way."

To many readers this would seem to be, as it did to me originally, nothing more than "just the old standard stuff for just another standard Indian holy man." But one thing that particularly impressed me about

David Loye

Dadaji's message of love was how it not only accounted for Peter's great affinity for him but also, in India, in supposedly a radically different culture, it dovetailed with both Riane's work and my enthusiasm for the Darwin who wrote of love 95 times in *The Descent of Man*.

Like almost all other religions, Hinduism is a distressing mix of dominator as well as partnership elements. But Dadaji was, as was Jesus, expressing a rejection of the dominator model and advocating a shift to the partnership model.

Most interesting was this prediction. To paraphrase Peter's account of what Dadaji had said, "The Indian authorities say the Kali Yuga will last thousands of years. But I say it will end beginning in 1989. This will open a time when people will no longer seek the guru to lead them, but will follow the guru within."

In Hindu philosophy human evolution takes place in a succession of phases or yugas, of which the Kali Yuga is the worst and the Krita Yuga is the best. In effect Dadaji was saying that the dominator-model-driven period of wars and exploitation and other ills that had transformed so much of the twentieth century into a nightmare rather than the fulfillment of earlier dreams would begin to come to an end in 1989.

This prediction was in the 1970's. I found it fascinating that, out of the joint search for peace initiated by Mikhail Gorbachev, to which conservative president Ronald Reagan had responded, it was indeed in 1989 that the Berlin Wall separating East and West Germany was torn down—an act that came to symbolize not merely the fall of the Soviet Union but the ending of the Cold War and the rise of hope for humanity to reach a new level of evolution.

Dadaji further seemed to be saying that ahead lay a time when people would no longer wander about like sheep in search of a shepherd or a sheep dog—or to follow those who became the Hitlers or their potential successors of this earth, to bark, bite, and bamboozle or slaughter the rest of us like sheep. Rather, he was saying, we would be guided by the wisdom of nature, God, or Goddess within us.

History, alas, has not borne this out. Nonetheless, the burgeoning of civil society – of thousands of grassroots movements worldwide for peace, human rights (including increasingly women's rights and children's rights), and environmental balance attest to the new consciousness Dadaji predicted.

On digging deeper through discussions with Peter, I was thunderstruck by how the ancient Hindu vision of how the evolution of ourselves and this earth unfolds corresponded point for point both with the modern macrohistorical view for which Riane gained her entry into the Old Boy's Club of Adam Smith, Marx, Sorokin, and so on, and with the pattern I had discerned in the neglected parts of Darwin.

The theory of the Yugas begins with a stage of innocence for our species, the original Golden Age of the Satya Yuga. This was followed by a steady decline rather than an ascendency, as most of us have been taught and have believed in the West. First came the decline in how to live in harmony with the reality of ourselves, and nature, and the universe, which over thousands of years has been called spirituality. This was the Silver Age of the Treta Yuga. Then came the further decline to the Copper Age of the Dvapara Yuga. And then came the drop into the Kali Yuga.

Of this Kali Yuga, one of the oldest sacred texts of India, the Vishnu Purana, says, "The leaders who rule over the Earth will be violent and seize the goods of their subjects...The leaders, with the excuses of fiscal need, will rob and despoil them... Moral values and the rule of the law will lessen from day to day until the world will be completely perverted."

Finishing this book following a century of the rise of Hitlers, Stalins, Pol Pots, and now the practice runs for would-be emulators is enough to make one shudder.

But then, according to the old belief, with the shift to the new Golden Age of the Krita Yuga, will come the elevation of humanity to a higher plane of existence.

I find myself thinking of many things. Of whether the cataclysmic rejection of Bush policies in the 2006 elections in America could possibly again foreshadow the long hungered for, but long delayed shift to the Krita Yuga. But more so, I find myself thinking of how the older I get the more I am impressed with the stream of an intelligence in common that age after age, in thinker after thinker, seeks not only to surface but to take abiding hold.

It is as if a stream of the cumulated wisdom for our species hovers in consciousness somewhere above us. Most of the time, for most of us, soon after we are born a great mass of brambles and shrubbery grows up alongside the stream to conceal it from us. For all of us, at least once in a lifetime, we stumble upon a break in the shrubbery, and for a second or two we see the stream. Then frightened, we pull back into life as it was and is supposed to be.

But given the glimpse, those who advance human evolution persist in tearing back the shrubbery to reveal the stream to others—and when they are crucified, co-opted, or otherwise squashed, once safely dead and gone, they sometimes enter history as the inspirational figures whose names we are supposed to remember.

I think of how, under the guise of gaining better access to this stream through a huge investment in an amoral science and the wondrous gadgets of its technology, the 20th century did so much to close the gaps in the shrubbery and restrict sight of the stream.

And I think of what is again and again expressed by readers of *The Chalice and the Blade* who write to Riane, or come up after one of her talks, to tell her of their feelings. Before the book was published we had been concerned it would meet with incomprehension as well as heavy opposition. But what we were to hear over and over again was this.

"What you say is something I have always known in my heart. Thank you for expressing it."

Soon we were brought to Germany for Riane to meet with Goudevert and other Volkswagen officials and VIPs involved in his International Partnership Initiative. We were put up in the Volkswagen guest house in Wolfsburg, the tiny German town close to the border between West and East Germany where Volkswagen is headquartered. Thus we explored a prospective cross-Atlantic collaboration around the partnership vision.

One of the best parts was the friendship that developed between Peter, Uta, and ourselves. We journeyed together through the marvelous old feudal towns, walked through the beautiful woods surrounding Wolfsburg, then leafing into the warm, moist life of Spring. We celebrated Peter's April 25th and my April 26th birthdays in a simultaneous little ceremony replete with Bach, cake, and glasses raised to wild toasts with wine. At one point we journeyed with them high into the mountains of the Black Forest to a resort, at another point, the two of them visited us in Carmel. Soon Peter and Uta had formed and were teaching their own partnership education group in Wolfsburg while Peter began to explore the possibilities of launching a partnership education movement throughout Germany.

One of his many friends at high levels—for on top of everything else, in the Herr Doktor Professor persona, Peter chaired two extremely important committees for the integration of science, technology, and education in regional economic development—was Professor Rita Seussmuth, then president of the German Parliament, the Bundestag.

This was a post equivalent in status to Vice President of the U.S. Professor Seussmuth had become such an enthusiast of *Kelch und Schwert* that she organized a conference for governmental officials and department heads to provide Riane with a platform from which to explain the book and its implications for the future.

We were driven from Wolfsburg at the far eastern edge of West Germany all the way across the country to Bonn (then the capital of West Germany) in the far western edge by Volkswagen limousine. We spent the night in a fine hotel at German government expense. Then at the crack of dawn we were whisked away in a long black Mercedes with chauffeur to Professor Suessmuth's palatial government mansion on the banks of the Rhine.

As together we stood on the veranda overlooking the grand sweep of the Rhine, awaiting Professor Suessmuth's arrival, I marveled at how here I was, a boy from a little oil town in Oklahoma, and here beside me was Riane, by the time I was in high school a Jewish refugee fleeing for her life from the Nazi terror in Austria. And here were the two of us standing there in the home of the second highest official in the German government, with Riane shortly to address influentials and other people in government who Professor Seussmuth hoped might help her build the greater Germany of Suessmuth's personal vision.

We heard a call of delight from behind us and into the breakfast room she swept. Rita Suessmuth was a short, wiry, cheery, woman of middle-age, clad in a brisk tweed business jacket and skirt. She had the direct and honest gaze and clasp of hand that immediately told you here was not just an important person. Here was one of the rare ones you could trust. She motioned us to the breakfast table and its delightful assortment of drinkables and munchables. She began to immediately talk of her enthusiasm for the book. Suddenly the phone rang. Up she jumped.

"That's Eastern Europe," she said. "It's a national radio hook-up," she explained.

She laughed, then collected her thoughts.

"Please excuse me for a few minutes. I am going to tell all of Eastern Europe about *The Chalice and The Blade*," she said as she lifted the receiver to take the call in a nearby nook off the breakfast room.

As later that day I sat in the large conference room with Professor Seussmuth and Riane at the dias, and then as the forum got underway, I came to see how it all fitted together.

To begin with, I was understandably thrilled to see this level of respect for Riane's work—to see this level of belief that the power of her work might change history here in the heart of the land that had been poisoned by the terror that so strongly motivated her and also me. Most immediately, on the political level, Seussmuth faced the problem of being a woman in a notably male-dominant society. Here, by sheer force of mind and character, both in her political party and in the government, she had become second in command to the orotund presence and voice of the Chancellor Helmut Kohl, not only male but physically about twice her size.

Suessmuth's strength lay primarily in her ability to win a large number of women voters for the party in elections. In regard to the book, Riane's gender and the stature that Seussmuth asserted and certified for it further strengthened her own appeal to women voters. But far beyond this was her grasp, as I saw it, of the potential of this book for helping her in her own personal campaign to bury the male-dominant authoritarianism that had made possible Hitler in Germany. I saw that she could see Riane's book held the potential to help liberate the partnership model that had been embodied in the thinking and tradition of so many of Germany's greatest minds—Goethe, Heine, Kant, Herder, Lessing, Schiller at their best, as well as Marx and Engels originally, before despairing of gaining their goal any other way led them to embrace the disastrous idea of a "dictatorship of the proletariat."

Here was a book by a Jewish scholar forced to flee Hitler as a child, returned to her homeland at a time of the great push by the good Germans to assuage their guilt and put the shame of the Nazis beyond them. Peter, who had grown up as a boy protected by the fact that he was not a Jew, was eloquent on the degree to which he, as well as many others, felt this guilt even though they were only children at the time. It was a book, further, that put the tragedy of Germany, and thereby so much of the rest of the world during the mid-twentieth century, within the sweep of a new perspective on human evolution—a perspective that provided, for the first time, an adequate explanation of what had happened, as well as how it might be prevented from ever happening again.

Rita spoke, Riane spoke, there was applause and some signs of enthusiasm. I could hope, we all could hope. But we left inevitably wondering how much of this would "take" in the face of all the old poison still embedded in the system.

3,000 Years of Love

We returned to Germany a few years later, again financed by Volkswagen. Riane was to be the main speaker to the chief annual gathering that would pull in from the cities of all continents the top managers of the hundreds of branches and agencies for Volkswagen worldwide. This was to serve Goudevert's drive to liberalize and humanize Volkswagen operations globally, as well as influence other industries and the communities in which Volkswagen was a respected and important presence—for Goudevert was one of those rare good leaders of great vision who emerge and prevail for a time here and there, which give one a wan hope for the spread of multi-nationals that might help bring on a better world.

But suddenly came the word from Peter that a dreadful thing had happened. Because of a downturn in sales for Volkswagen and other financial troubles, a dominator of dominators had deposed Goudevert as Chairman. Indeed, Goudevert was departing the company, leaving behind in command the authoritarian son of one of the industrialists who had not only been close to the Nazis; he had apparently been a key player in the early financing of their rise to power as well as the success of Hitler's war machine.

We expected both Riane's talk and Goudevert's International Partnership Initiative would be canceled, but neither happened. It must have been that this talk by some woman was to the new leader of not enough importance to bother with amid the drastic changes he was forcing across to up the profits and reassure the stockholders.

Again we were flown to Germany. Again we were zipped around in limousines, put up in the finest hotel, and taken to the meeting chamber where a throng of Volkswagen managers assembled from around the world were sitting, row after row.

David Loye

Out from the bright lighted stage rose the dias for the speaker, constructed in such a way that psychologically it seemed to make of the speaker a figure twenty feet tall, illumined within the blaze of a single powerful spotlight from above. Given the strikingly youthful beauty of Riane as she stepped into that light, hovering there, no doubt many must have wondered how a woman who looked so young could actually have been a refugee from the Nazis. Her powerful delivery had a stunning effect, however, in more ways than one.

Peter's informal survey afterward found that what seemed to be a majority of the wives of the Volkswagen managers were very enthusiastic. The bulk of the men, however, either didn't know what to make of it or were wrathful to find this "feminist stuff" being shoved at them.

One sympathetic Volkswagen manager, of an agency in Hong Kong I recall, told us of afterward being in the elevator with some women. The women were talking favorably and heartily about the talk, but in the elevator also happened to be the new chairman's wife. Making a face of disgust, she strongly conveyed her disapproval of the talk and the message that those who expected themselves or their husbands to be favored by her or her husband had better drop this ill-begotten enthusiasm. So ended the Volkswagen partnership venture—and at the time, seemingly also the partnership venture in Germany.

But a decade later, both Peter Meyer-Dohm and Rita Suessmuth were still on board, and Riane and I traveled to Germany once again. Riane was again to share the podium with Professor Suessmuth, this time at the famous Rahthaus in Berlin—to which I will return.

Both Riane and I have written at length of the systems dynamics that like a sick tree produces the poisoned apples of events that suddenly reverse the partnership direction for human evolution The picture is of how in order to preserve a sick system against the mounting challenges to its existence—e.g., the challenge of the 18th century Enlightenment, the American revolution, and now the rapidly escalating progressive movements in which the two of us along with millions of others still living today have been and are still involved—this Thing has spawned a brood of Hydras. And mewling, still half blind, motivated only to gobble up whatever lies in their path, these fledgling monsters are groping to find their way from the nest.

As thousands of scholars and other intelligent and caring people around the world have come to see—as I've touched on here from time to time—one can perhaps most easily glimpse this in the surface symptoms of American presidential elections. Thus in the U.S. there is this sense of the Thing gradually, surely, inexorably escalating in the sequence of the Nixon, Reagan, Bush I, and as I write now, the Bush II triumph of corporatism and fundamentalism basking in the moral bankruptcy of the Republican party and the political bankruptcy of the Democratic party.

It is what one senses at work behind the buy-up of governments by Big Oil, Big Coal, and Big Lumber. The bilking of the multitude by Big Energy, Big Communications, and Big Utility. The pollution and destruction of the environment by Big Chemical, Big Car, and Big Oil Tanker. The seizure, dumbing down, and enslavement of minds by Big Media and Big Entertainment. The buy-up of Big, Little, and Organic Food by Big Tobacco. The slurping-up and exploitation of the world's water by Big Water.

But at the same time, rising in tandem with the shove backward is the counter-cultural thrust of nothing less than the life force itself. There rises this vision expressed by the best of our species, embodied in the key events and movements that have fitfully shoved us ahead.

There is the enduring fact that it is up to us to move our species ahead, and that our efforts, be they large or small, do make the difference.

I tried to capture this in a poem I wrote for one of Riane's birthdays called "Boats with Sails of Fire."

Boats with Sails of Fire

> As in a dream, as in a boat with sails of fire, I saw us
> in motion above the ocean.
>
> It was as if we had become the high up swallow at sunset
> still climbing the air, its wings still aflame, but for us
> there was no hovering point, only this steady flight
> westward, Pacific ocean giving way to Indian ocean,
> giving way to Atlantic ocean, ever toward the dawn.
>
> I saw our exhilaration, how joyful we were to be there
> soaring still aflame with the sun, while steadily below and
> behind us gently spread a gentle darkness over all the earth.
>
> But then the sail rope went limp to the hand.
> On there ahead and rapidly nearing came the booming of
> the old thunder and the saber dance of the old lightning, for
> there it was again, the great moiling and billowing pack of
> the old, old clouds, and I felt our despair—to look down.
> And feel the winds of faith desert us.
>
> (continued)

3,000 Years of Love

To look down into the dark, waiting maw of the hungry sea, and feel now how swiftly we could plunge into it with no one to see or, as time droned by, to even care.

We were alone, so terribly alone.

But then with the uncanny beauty of pelicans rising into flight—each very, very thinly spread out over the water but now by eyesight at last linked together by knowledge of each other, ocean by ocean and climbing into the bright air over the pockets of the seas—I saw all those in boats like ours rising or already risen.

As far as we could sail and eye could see, there they were, rising out of the darkness of land and water to pursue the dawn in boats with sails of fire.

TWENTY
THE MARCH ON MOSCOW AND MARRIAGE

I must, with much else to do yet, begin to close down this book. As Robert Frost once put something of this constraint so beautifully,

> The woods are lovely, dark and deep.
> But I have promises to keep,
> And miles to go before I sleep,
> And miles to go before I sleep.

So at this juncture in our lives together, what else shall I write of?

The good times with our children over the years, six in all, Jenella, Kathryn, Chris and Jon for me, Andrea and Lori for Riane? As one grows older, that peak of pleasure, of grandchildren, Evan, Chris, Kenny and Jase for me, Dashiell, Julia, Matt and Cami for Riane. Or for me, my sisters Nan and Wendy. Or for Riane, the beloved Eli, Nuscha and Rudi for the tiny remnant still left of her family out of the Holocaust and the toll of time.

Kari Norgaard who co-authored with us the Center for Partnership Studies's report *Women, Men, and the Global Quality of Life?* This was our CPS statistical study showing that the status of women can b e a better predictor of general quality of life than even GDP. The

3,000 Years of Love

intermittent stream of beautiful, brilliant, and remarkable people from here and elsewhere throughout the world, all out to do good in this world, many succeeding, thank goodness, who over the years have poured in and out of our house for a meal, or afternoon, or evening? The awards and honors, particularly for Riane? Mexico and that magnificent great black ironwork sculpture of a rearing horse that I, alas, persuaded her not to buy for $1000, which would have been worth at least $100,000 today? The glory of Ravello and Amalfi, of Dubrovnick, of the magnificent beaches, mountains, and valleys it has been our joy to visit together?

Back and forth, back and forth life goes. So also went our life from the private sphere to the public sphere and then back from the public to the private, as Riane would say. Out of all this back to me now comes how we came to marry.

During the closing years of the Cold War, what I persist in thinking of as "the March on Moscow" was an important historical event for both the peace movement and the feminist movement.

Actually, this is a typical distortion of what memory does to us as we grow older.

"That's not it at all," Riane said in reading these pages. My revised title for it would now be something like "The Scandinavian Women's March for Peace," which she would insist is still not right.

In any case, as this indicates, it was a move launched by an alliance of Swedish, Norwegian, Danish and Finnish women. The group had already crossed the Atlantic to descend on Washington, D.C. It was now going to "cross the frozen wastes" to descend on Leningrad to put pressure on the governments of both East and West to end the insanity that, while both sides sat there frozen in opposition, continued to put the whole world at risk with enough nuclear missile power at the ready to blow up a good chunk of the earth and its people if the other blinked.

Riane had been invited as one of three U.S. delegates to join the group.

"They're going to meet in Helsinki and then go by train to Leningrad," she said.

As more times than one would ever guess has been my role, I did everything I could to persuade her not to go, but this was a lost cause from the beginning. Was I to join the forces of cowardice and indifference? How could I possibly not support the idea? The situation put her in the role of the courageous and socially responsible activist and me in the role of the fat head obstructionist nay-sayer.

As the time for departure neared, her attention shifted from the noble and exciting venture ahead to anxiety about her daughters, her work, and me.

It was hard to believe the Soviets would imprison them or do anything else drastic of that sort, but one never knew. And one never knew whether some deranged Cold War warrior of either their side, or our side, might try to blow up the train, or to shoot the women, for these things did not simply happen in movies.

If anything were to happen to her, she had three concerns. One was her children—she made me promise I would in effect become both father and mother to her daughters.

Next was the book to which she had already given nearly ten years of her life: *The Chalice and the Blade*—still unpublished then. She handed me the manuscript with a look that was both a question and an appeal, yet with the hard edge of firm expectation. She made me promise that if anything happened I would somehow push this precious

3,000 Years of Love

book into print.

The third item was me.

"I can't bear to think about it," she said.

I knew what she meant without further words. That life could be so cruel as to cut short our time together was the horrible but inescapable thought. In book after book this was how the story ended.

I thought of long ago, when I was a boy in Oklahoma. The one person we all worshiped, young and old, was Will Rogers, the Cherokee Indian from Claremore who went on to worldwide become one of the most beloved Americans of his time.

The pictures were still fresh in my mind of Rogers standing alongside the one-eyed bush pilot Wiley Post as they posed for the joint news photo beside the Winnie Mae. This was the trusty plane, named after Wiley Post's wife, which had been financed by the richest man in our little town of Bartlesville, Frank Phillips, founder of Phillips Petroleum.

This was in itself a memory marker for me, as Frank Phillips' huge home occupied the whole next block to the block where I lived. So important were his movements to our neighborhood "gang" that we used to post lookouts on days when he might be expected to come walking past our house.

Up the cry would go, "Uncle Frank's coming!" Whereupon we would all flock to play next to the sidewalk, simpering and looking sweet. Though there was surely no one around to take a pot shot at him or try to kidnap him, he always walked with a Philipino body guard who looked like Odd Job in the James Bond movies. As he came abreast of us "Uncle Frank" would beam and from the box carried by his body guard take up and pass down to each of us a whole dollar bill.

David Loye

But there in mind they were, Will Rogers and Wiley Post, next to Uncle Frank's plane. In the picture they were waving as they set off to fly to Russia. The purpose for which the flight was funded was to open up a route for air mail to Russia, but within what had become Will Roger's role was something of a larger purpose. He had been appointed by President Roosevelt as first an ambassador of good will to South America. This then had unofficially widened to become the role in which this comedian and popular newspaper columnist, who had said "I never met a man I didn't like," was welcomed and even in many cases beloved everywhere, as America's Ambassador of Good Will to the World.

There they were standing in our minds when the devastating telegram came to fill the headlines of their crash and death together at Point Barrow, Alaska.

Was this what lay ahead for us?

No matter how noble or heroic the Scandinavian women's march on Leningrad might be, as far as I was concerned it was no justification for anything opening up such a risk. But her mind was made up. There was no persuading her otherwise, and she turned to practicalities.

If I was to be left behind, a comparatively penniless and aging writer with nothing to live on but social security and a small pension, she wanted to be sure I was well taken care of. But the legalities and practicalities of leaving money and property raised the tricky question of marriage.

For her, this would be no easy decision. The problems of her first marriage and her research and the feminist revolution had instilled in her a feeling of the anathema of the bondage implied by the old terms of husband and wife.

3,000 Years of Love

As for me, though I had no such deepset feeling, I was quite content to go on living together unmarried, as we had already for almost ten years. I also felt that in the best sense we had earlier married in our own way. A few months after we first met, while in the desert magic of Sedona, Arizona, we'd gone into one of the great red rock canyons and created our own marriage ceremony.

We worked up an informal service with a ritual involving the placing of sticks on a rock in a mystic pattern. I placed my camera on a rock nearby with the automatic self-ticking device whirring to provide us with a wedding picture. As I recall, there was a squirrel and a hawk on high for witness, and who knows, perhaps a prairie dog or two. And so we'd been married.

But now if it was to be done, it had to be done formally. We found a lovely woman preacher, Ann Swallow, out in Carmel Valley, who married us in her home, just us by ourselves, with no one else present. As we looked at each other, Riane spoke of her everlasting love for me. I read one of the poems I had originally written to her. And that was it. And she was off.

This left me with the manuscript of a book I was both eager to read and leery of doing so. Everything we had discussed or I had looked at along the way—particularly the implications of Minoan Crete and other centers of the prehistoric Goddess-worshiping partnership culture—presented the enticing prospect of at last seeing how she had managed to fit it all together.

But what if this pivotal book for her wasn't as good as she hoped it was? She had been up and down in mood about the book for years.

Sometimes she feared it was doomed for rejection by the male scientific establishment. Her experience with GERG fired her concern.

She was by now pals with and even collaborating on a paper with the leading Hungarian biologist Vilmos Csanyi, as well as good friends with the genial teddy bear economist Pennti Malaska from Finland, the comparably genial and teddy bear chaos theorist Ralph Abraham from nearby Santa Cruz, and the witty Harvard astrophysicist Eric Chaisson. But other than Laszlo who recognized her brilliance early, others were still leery of her—as well as anything to do with the women's movement or feminism.

Sometimes she also feared the book would be seen by feminist scholars as too action oriented and by feminist activists as too scholarly. She also worried she had bit off too much for a single book—that it would be rejected by both the vital acquiring editor for a publisher and then if published it would be rejected by readers as just too much to digest in a single book.

So unsure was she of the book's reception she was beginning to doubt whether it was practical for her to go on pinning her hopes on a career as a writer.

It would be a dreadful blow to accept the idea—for she had not only given up her law practice and everything else to sink her life, money to support herself while writing, and all her aspirations into this book. Into this book, in order to somehow arrive at and provide others with the answer to the question of where and how our species had gone off track, and how to get back on track again to the better future, she had invested year after year in research in archeology, mythology, anthropology, and 35,000 years of prehistory and history. Atop all that she had mastered the intricacies of systems science and chaos theory.

She had further riding on it the expectations of our friends in GERG and the need to prove to everyone else she was someone to be reckoned with both as a scholar and as an original thinker. Was it all a balloon of illusion about to be punctured?

Looking back on that time, I think that way down underneath all the other reasons she had for wanting to join the march on Leningrad was that it would be a relief to get halfway around the world from the sink or swim pressure the book was putting on her now that it was sufficiently finished to face its first reader.

So with my realization of all this working in me I picked it up and began to read. And was soon entranced. And as thousands and by now millions of other readers, I read on, and on, and on.

I thought of the power of Karl Marx to cut through to the core of social and historical dynamics, of Will and Ariel Durant's ability to make history come to life, of an over-all compassion for which I searched unsuccessfully in mind for a comparable predecessor. This book, I felt then and still do, was of that order of accomplishment. But beyond all that, it was also something new and vitally needed for the 20th century.

It was a voice of balance out of a prolonged time of imbalance, of health out of sickness, of sanity out of insanity.

Sitting alone in bed there while she was 6,000 miles away in Leningrad, this was the manuscript I read on, page after page, marveling at what Riane had created.

TWENTY-ONE
WHO AM I?

And who or what else should I write of here, in closing down?

After writing of Riane and so many others with some intimacy, should I not write a bit more of one other?

Because of all I have yet to do I am not likely to live long enough, nor do I have the motivation, to write an autobiography. And as I find myself haunted by the question of trauma in childhood, and how it shapes our lives, should I not at least touch on this in regard to my own life?

So who really am I?

Who am I, who out of love for Riane, and love for love itself, can write this book. But as for love for oneself, I remain equivocal, basically unable to love myself.

It isn't that I hate or even dislike myself. I wholeheartedly like what I am and have made of myself. But I find myself incapable of saying I can love myself.

If it began in trauma, as of course it did, what was the trauma in my life akin to the trauma for Riane, or for that matter, akin to the trauma for the rest of us?

Ever more clearly I see that basically it was what has maimed most of us. It was the trauma of being born a creature of the Flame, programmed to live according to the Partnership Way, but born into a world still encased in the cold, hard arms of the Glacier extending down from the North and up from the South of the psyche as well as our planet.

It was the trauma of being born into a world over 5,000 years programmed to function according to the Dominator Way.

To reinforce this basic programming there is of course always the booster shot administered by what happens to us—that is, to a specific person in a specific environment at a specific time, which differs and yet so often deep down under is the same for each of us.

For Riane it was the trauma of going one day from being a happy little person in a seemingly secure and welcoming world to being the Jew for hunting down like an animal. But what was it personally for me?

Nothing so drastic on the surface. But when you are small and new to this world the difference in scale for what to the adult eye is a minor trauma can loom within the nightmare world of the child buried within each of us as huge and fearful, straining within us to remain beyond memory.

In *Brave Laughter* I have written of what I came to feel had been the devastating impact not only of my mother's lack of love, but her active opposition, and her drive for absolute control—which I've come to find was the mother-child relational pattern for a surprising number of my friends and others I've met.

There are the glimpses into the core of the pain that the self-protective controller within each of us, which Freud called "the censor," has now and then released to me in poems I've written Riane.

For instance,

David Loye

The Wall of Glass

They say if you are ever
to be whole and healed you
must learn to love yourself.
But I know I cannot.
And I know you cannot.
There were just too many
times, and places, and years
of living naked and yearning
outside the wall of glass.
Too many years then of
living chilled and unloving
within the wall of glass.
Too many years of that brittle
world of unlove, of feeling all
about us the frantic fingers and
hearing all about us the screams
frozen within the glacier of
5000 years encasing all of us.
I find I can only love you,
as you love me, and this is
our wholeness and our healing.
For in the radiance of the fire
and in our naked life together behind
the wall of glass we are as one.
And in loving you, and you loving
me, we can through this love tunnel
to each other to at least feel the glow
of what it might be to love ourselves.

In searching for an answer to the deep unsettling and the pain, however, mainly there comes back to me one grey afternoon in the dead of winter in Minnesota.

I was five. There were ten or eleven of us tobogganing in a park. For an hour or so we had been flinging ourselves on those sleek long wedded planks with curved front called toboggans to go shooting down a deep snow-encrusted hill.

Then an older boy arrived with an idea that greatly excited us. He would set two of the toboggans side by side at the top of the hill. He told us little fellows to split up and get on the two toboggans. Then amid great merriment on all sides he picked up the guide ropes for both toboggans, and standing up, straddling the two toboggans with a foot on the back of each of them, with a whoop he set us shooting down the slope in tandem.

Against the blast of wind and the ice crystals being churned up, I had shut my eyes. I was second from the front on my toboggan. The first boy saw the tree and jumped. But I didn't. I simply shot forward into his empty slot to smack the tree full force with my head.

I woke to find a handful of playmates standing over me, looking down in concern. I felt strange, horribly frightened but of what I didn't know. It was getting dark. I only knew I should be getting home. One boy tried to help me up but enraged I shook him off.

"I can get up by myself!"

I had a bad headache and all I could think of was getting home.

As I set off, one little boy fell in beside me.

We crossed the street at one point and he headed off in another direction. Then he stopped.

"Where are you going?" he said.

David Loye

"I'm going home."

"That's not the right direction. It's this way. You live next door to me."

"You're crazy," I said.

He stood there and watched me for a while as I continued on my way, then shook his head and went on toward his home.

Now that I was alone the fear deepened and widened. It was completely dark by now. All one could see street after street were the wan lights of winter at each corner. And the lights in the windows of houses. But all of seemed set back miles from the street where I was.

It was that early time of night, around suppertime, when everybody had come home from work or play and so there were no longer any cars moving anywhere that I remember. Street after street after street seemed empty of all life or movement.

It was if in all of the silent, cold, and alien spread of Minneapolis there was just myself, this increasingly fierce headache, the sullen chill of the Minnesota night working in through my mittens, coat and snow boots, the rage, and the fear, and the crunch of my feet on the dirty snow and ice of the sidewalk that seemed to just go on and on and on. Where was my house?

At last I saw it!

I began to run, feeling it was safe to cry now. There it was at last!

I ran up the steps to the porch and seized the door knob, but it wouldn't turn. Sobbing now, crying out, I fought at it, trying to turn the knob. It was locked!

I rushed to the big living room window just right of the door, and then the horror full force hit me. The living room was dark. In fact, the whole house was dark.

3,000 Years of Love

I pressed my face to the glass and everything that up to that point had sustained me over my short life dropped into nowhere, for there was nothing in the living room.

All I could make out in the thin soup of the cold winter's afterlight was the outline of the empty fireplace. The rug, the divan, the chairs, all of it, everything was gone.

I pressed my face to the glass, and squinted and squinted, but nowhere could I see back there where the kitchen was, and they would be eating supper, so much as a sliver or atom of light.

What had happened to them? My father, my mother, my two little sisters—had they been taken away by the police?

Had they all been killed in some mysterious way—for the world of the child, filled everywhere with mystery, still contains the possibilities we come to rule out later on as highly unlikely.

It was the years of the Great Depression of the 1930s, of which as the oldest child I was aware from observing my parents' fear. Had they lost the house because they couldn't pay the rent—for my father had been out of work for a long time, and this was the fear I'd heard them talk of.

Soon I didn't care. All I knew was that I was hungry, and cold, and in pain, and needed to eat, and be comforted, and was increasingly mad at them beyond containment because they weren't there.

And then the surreality that can take over the universe from a dreadful blow to the head provided what seemed to be the only reasonable answer. They had simply gone off and left me.

They had decided they didn't want me any more.

It was what I had long feared, never from my father, but of my mother I was never sure. Somehow she had prevailed and I was now alone on this earth in the dead of a Minnesota's winter night.

And there was nowhere I knew of to go.

I set off blindly walking through the snow drifts. There was nothing left to do but hope that somewhere out there in the night I would find some place or someone to take me in.

I do not know how long it was, but out of walking, and walking, and walking I suddenly saw the familiar gleam of the radiator and elegant green body of our old Packard. It was my father out looking for me. He took me home and I was fed and put to bed and the doctor called.

For several days afterward, I was special. They came to see me in my bed—my grandparents in from the outskirts of Minneapolis, and my uncles Tully and Evan over from St.Paul, even some curious playmates from the new neighborhood.

For that is what had happened. Two weeks before we had moved from our old house to a new house in a new neighborhood close to the park where I'd hit the tree. But through the amnesia that can follow a serious concussion, such as I'd suffered, I had blanked out on the change, and on that night I had walked across the city to the empty old home.

It seems like nothing now, to set on paper like this. But over the years I've come to know that deep within the lives of many, if not all of us—the details changed, but not the essence—one finds more or less the same story.

The difference the trauma makes in our lives depends on whether there was enough love there both before and after it happened to begin to heal it. And whether in the end we are sufficiently mobilized by joy and gratitude for the gift of life under almost any circumstances to transcend it.

TWENTY-TWO
THE DARK VISITOR RETURNS

And so came the day that all of us fear and year after year seek to put off. The day the world ends in mind before it comes to an end in actuality. The day of the arrival of the dark visitor, no stranger by then, come to at last, let us hope, call us home. But more probably to call us—we fear or with reluctance accept—to oblivion. Or worse, to call away the one we love.

Riane had been bleeding and suffering severe pain. The trouble, the tests showed, was in her uterus. It was full of blood. She tried a myriad of holistic approaches to no avail. Though the cause of the bleeding was unknown, the tests revealed the worst of all possibilities.

There would have to be an operation. There was no reason for her to fear, she was told. With luck—and luck was often on our side these days, she was told—the operation would do it.

All very well. And of course one smiled, and knew for the benefit of others that it was all going to work out just fine. But still . . .

It was in April of 1996. While outwardly, for the benefit of both of us, I said what one says to express the conviction that of course once again we would put off the arrival of the dark visitor, privately I turned again to poetry.

David Loye

That I Could Lose You

That I could lose you—
the terror is beyond reckoning,
imagining, consoling.
Could one ever find compensation
for the loss of a universe?
That one day there should be
this vast hole, this void,
this emptiness in all of
space and time and whatever
else there was and is
before space and time?
Could roof, and walls, and
door be blown off the house
and the child gazing into
the black heart of the tornado
ever, ever be comforted again?

I saw and felt what only poetry has ever begun to express adequately. I felt what Dylan Thomas captured with those lines

> Do not go gentle into that good night.
> Rage, rage against the dying of the light.

Or Wordsworth, in that most haunting of great poems once one fully absorbs what lies behind it, what had happened to him—as it must happen to most of us at one time or another in our lives.

3,000 Years of Love

> Surprised by joy—impatient as the Wind
> I turned to share the transport—Oh! with whom
> But Thee, deep buried in the silent tomb,
> That spot which no vicissitude can find?
> Love, faithful love, recalled thee to my mind—
> But how could I forget thee? Through what power,
> Even for the least division of an hour,
> Have I been so beguiled as to be blind
> To my most grievous loss?—That thought's return
> Was the worst pang that sorrow ever bore,
> Save one, one only, when I stood forlorn,
> Knowing my heart's best treasure was no more;
> That neither present time, nor years unborn
> Could to my sight that heavenly face restore.

Over the days that I waited back to me came three memories of the dark visitor's earlier arrivals. The first came before I knew her, in the total collapse, when she had gone from doctor to doctor.

Back to my mind came the curious story she once told me about that time, how finally, in desperation, she decided to leave her housekeeper in charge of her home and daughters to seek refuge in some healing retreat.

She called several well-known places but could find none that had openings.

"Even when I told them I was desperate and did they know of any other places, some were unbelievably abrupt and cold."

She finally called the number for the Self-Realization Fellowship founded by the famous Parahansa Yogananda, author of *The Autobiography of a Yogi.*

"They not only immediately accepted me, but were so much warmer and more considerate than all the rest. I have never forgotten it."

There was an opening at the Self-Realization Fellowship ashram on the coast at Encinitas. Again, she was both surprised and deeply touched by the exceptionally warm reception she received.

There was some kind of regular ceremony that normally one could not attend until one had been there for some prescribed period of time. To this she was immediately admitted. Soon after her arrival she was visited by the robed, stately, elderly woman they simply called Mother whom Yogananda himself had put in charge of the Encinitas ashram.

Moved by the unusual warmth and caring that emanated from this woman, Riane broke down and wept and was embraced and held as a mother would a child. She was told to just rest, and eat their good food, and walk in the garden, and whenever she felt like it she could come see this Mother and they would talk.

Toward the end of her stay, as she came to recognize she was receiving an unusual amount of caring personal attention, she finally asked the question that had been building in her mind.

"Why have you been so good to me? I have felt—special."

"We were told you would come. We have been waiting for you."

Pointing to the portrait of Yogananda on the wall behind her, the head of the ashram went on. "Yogananda told us we must take special care of you. You have important work ahead."

Riane had accepted these words gratefully. But being the skeptic she is, she was not convinced they really meant what they implied. She and I had gone back and forth about it when she told me of this one day as we drove in Malibu near the striking oasis of another Self-Realization ashram on a lake.

Was it really possible that, years beforehand, her arrival in need had been predicted, that they'd been mystically primed in advance to help? Because of the studies during the Neuropsychiatric Institute basement years of that larger world of mystery within which we float like leaves on a river, and because of all I have since then extensively explored and experienced, I feel by now it could have been true.

Who is to say where the boundaries of this universe we move through begin and end?

The second memory was of how back in the earliest days of our life together, overcoming her great reluctance, I persuaded Riane to simply sit in a room with me and "Mr.Spock"—that is, the psychic diagnostician with whom I worked in our basement sessions at the Neuropsychiatric Institute, Barry Taff. All I asked was that she sit there and let him answer my questions.

So I asked Taff to focus on her and tell me what he thought her main health problem was.

I had told him nothing personal about her, nor did he ask, for that would have been going against the way we had learned we must operate.

He closed his eyes, put himself in a light trance, and then in his customary barking way of talk in rapid fire gave this diagnosis.

"You were in a car accident. You suffered a whiplash injury. This gave you two serious dislocations."

He darted a hand to the back of his neck.

"Here," he said.

He darted his other hand to a place along the spine in the lower back.

"And here," he said.

He then settled back and was silent.

"You pick up nothing of a possible heart problem?" I asked, for this was our chief fear at the time.

"No," he said. "Absolutely not."

"You are sure?"

"Yes, beyond question. I am particularly sensitive to heart problems, and I pick up nothing."

"And there is nothing else?"

"Only some problems with the stomach," he said. "The lining is worn out."

At the time this was only one more piece of information, one more opinion of many—one more guess most likely, because of the source, to be discounted or forgotten. Yet it foreshadowed the startling confirmation that was to come.

The third memory came from later.

"I haven't said much about this," she said to me one day after we had been in Carmel for about two years. "You know I love you. But I am in such continual stomach pain that I really don't know whether I want to go on living any more."

At the time I had been quite ill myself with the regular doctors able to come up with no clear diagnosis. Hearing of a chiropractor in nearby Pacific Grove with a reputation as an unusual healer, she had phoned to be met with the receptionist's firm "Dr. Jarvis is overloaded and can see no new patients." However, somehow she managed to get him to see me, as I remember—although she disagrees—by calling him directly and pleading that "medical science has given up on this man."

As I lay there on his table and he turned, and pulled, and tapped at me, he was chattering merrily about the kinds of things he encountered in all kinds of patients. Personally convinced there was little basically wrong with me, but greatly concerned about Riane, I kept pointing to her and saying "That sounds exactly like what *she's got.*"

Finally he succumbed, motioning me off and her onto the table.

"Let's see."

As he ran his hands gently down her back and felt of her skull and tugged at a leg, she began to unload her entire medical history in a torrent of words.

"Stop!" he said. "Your body tells me everything. You have had practically every symptom and been to practically every doctor there is."

He rattled both symptoms and specialists off with astounding accuracy. Then he said this.

Her problem, he said, was basically a fundamental dislocation in two places that in interacting had been throwing her whole system out of balance for years. This had brought on a condition so complex and difficult to deal with he had only seen it once before—in a tennis player who he felt would have died had she not come to him at the right time. He would need to see Riane once a week for a year, but this should do it with only an occasional visit thereafter.

This proved to be exactly correct.

As the weeks progressed and my understanding of chiropractics increased, I came to see he was gently encouraging the complex of muscles, nerves, and bones of her back and neck into correct or natural alignment, over and over gently realigning them as they slipped back toward the debilitating displacement.

And the two places of displacement he pointed to that were the physical cause of it all?

Precisely the two points that Barry Taff had pointed to years earlier.

But now, after all the torment over the years to her body and mind that she had managed to transcend, was this surgery to be the end? Why had the dark visitor returned? Why did our lives now literally hang on a surgeon's report?

Yet after twenty years of the healing power of love—for all sentiment or illusion aside, that is clearly what mainly kept the dark visitor from our door—now he had returned. It wasn't just the power of our love for one another. It was, I felt, the power of love as the force within and beyond us out of a mighty unfolding of the universe asserting itself through her. Now, after all this, what would they find? Was it all to come to an end?

As anyone knows who has been through this, the days of waiting are like years. But years quite unlike the years of normal reality. Years that are no longer filled with anything of consequence or meaning. Years devoid of content. Disoriented, not quite sure one is all here, empty, but seemingly endless years.

And so the day came. And the hour. And the phone call...

Another One Hundred Years

> Another one hundred years!
> That's all I could think of.
> After the waiting, the need
> to show no worry, to smile
> and carry on as though our
> world together did not dangle
> upon the lab report—this
> judgement of our time to rival
> formerly that of God, or Inquisitor,
> or some Last Court of Appeal.

(continued)

3,000 Years of Love

The phone call was to come at two.
It did not come by two-thirty.
Nor by three, nor by three-thirty.
And then. . .

Another one hundred years!
That's all I can think of—
and gratitude to something
somewhere that has decided this
is not the time.

We walked by the ocean. We worked in the garden. Soon that poem was followed by another.

A Single Rose

A single rose knows
what roses bunched
together however beautiful
cannot tell so well.

It is that love,
while multiple, has
a single voice at those times
when out of crisis
relief comes.

Such a rose I give to
you, now, today, at this

(continued)

David Loye

healing time after fear
beyond contemplation,
grateful that you
are here to receive it
and I to give it.

TWENTY-THREE
WHO ARE WE, AND WHERE ARE WE GOING?

Earlier, after high expectations in Germany seemed to come to an end with regression's triumph over partnership, I left off with only a mention of our later return to Germany—this time, in better circumstances, with Riane to share the podium with Professor Suessmuth in the famous and historically meaningful Rahthaus in Berlin.

This came in October, 2005, at the end point for a remarkable speaking tour for Riane. First we flew to Paris, and then we were driven to the posh resort town of Deauville on the coast. Here she was to address the 2005 Women's Economic Forum, a smaller but also prestigious version of the Barcelona Women's Forum she had addressed two years earlier.

It had been a few years since I had been in Europe. So back now all the difference that was Europe came, again fresh, exhilerating, exciting. Rather than tear down and improve with something worse, Deauville had been smart enough to hang onto its ancient charm. Driving in from Paris it began to signal what was coming with both villas and farmhouses still retaining the striking, old-style Normandy look. The tan stuccoed walls criss-crossed with dark brown planks, the high peaked roofs, the slender chimneys. Deauville itself turned out to be a jolly museum for the style with the old Normany look everywhere. We were to be housed in what appeared to be its most gay and boisterous old erection, the Normandy Deauville Hotel.

Of all the hotels I've been in, even on a short stay, I came to feel this was one of the most delightful. The rich red lobby, the flamboyant wallpaper in the halls, the bold flowered carpet underfoot, the figurines of angels, gnomes, owls, and cats of all kinds that festooned the high peaked roof line—it was something to which only Charles Dickens could have done justice. In keeping with the rest, the restaurant was of a storybook elegance. And to top it all was the casino attached by an ornate bridge.

The second day there, this casino was the site for an unforgettable soiree and banquet for all the speakers and forum attendees (who must have paid an enormous price for the event). All dressed in our best—the men in everything short of tails, the many more women, bright eyed, exuding delight, everywhere resplendent in their shimmering gowns—we milled about for a while in the kind of huge marbled hall lined with statues one only sees these days in movies of royal celebrations. This gave us time to get to know two wonderful women there, Lauralee Alben and Charlyn Beluzzi, who thereafter were to become treasured friends. Then on we all flowed into a comparably spectacular banquet hall for the comparably sumptuous meal.

Had this been most other places one would have expected the conference facility to be a considerable step down in style. But no, here, in contrast to the splendor of the 19th century at its most lavish, the Deauville Conference Center was everything the 21st century might hope for in a clean and soaring style that transcended the dreadful stuff that so often passed for modern during the 20th century. Outside it was a glistening white against the blue of the sky and the North Sea beyond the beach in the distance. Inside it was a marvel of a giant and sinuous white marble staircase with gleaming brass rail that led down into the cavern of the conference hall, with halls off to the sides for hors d'oeuvre and tasteful displays.

I will stop here: as the great romantic and prophetic poet William Blake once wrote, "Enough! Or too much."

As usual, Riane spoke to great effect. Some of the women—one of the most famous, in fact, who shall remain unnamed—were boring. Others I could see I would have found inspiring if I could have understood them. It was obviously a very important high level event for women who had infiltrated the top ranks of the corporate world to globally advance the women's movement along with their careers, but most were speaking French, which I couldn't understand. As I was trying to capture something of the event on a camcorder there was no time for the earphones and translation.

We next flew on to Switzerland and Zurich. This was to be the first of the five events that brought us back to Europe—the publication of three of our books in German. Riane's were *Die Kinder von Morgan,* a first German edition of *Tomorrow's Children,* with the face of a happy child upside down on the cover to catch the eye; and the new third German edition of *The Chalice and the Blade*, with my suggestion of Botticelli's painting of a nude Venus on the half shell on the cover.

Mine was *Darwin in Love,* with what I was billing on the internet as the first and only picture on record of Darwin smiling. This was a fetching cartoon I'd commissioned for the cover from my good friend, Carmel's great artist, cartoonist, and story teller Bill Bates. I thought the smile was perfect as it was just a touch tentative and anxious, with a roly poly Darwin with beard, a box of Valentine Day candy under one arm, and a bouquet of flowers in the other hand.

For me it was an occasion of considerable importance. After trying for years to get my Darwin books formally published in my own country, at last—in keeping with an unfortunately well-established pattern for anything in art or writing that runs counter to the market slots of the prevailing paradigm—they were gaining publication in Germany.

The Swiss event brought back memories of the earlier time when all over the U.S. and elsewhere little Centers for Partnership Education were simultaneously popping into being, self-organized, self-financed, and self-governed by hopeful good people animated by Riane's books, seeking to spread the Partnership Movement. It was primarily organized, with funding raised by a Swiss film-maker Martin Rausch and two gifted Swiss entrepreneurs, Suna Yamaner and Regula Langemann. With his German collaborator, the genial, media-wise Claus Biegart, Rausch had earlier visited us in Carmel to film Riane for a huge film project the two of them were engaged in floating. Now they'd scheduled us to speak and then interact with a panel of leading Swiss writers, intellects, and activists, with a book signing afterward.

Zurich itself went by almost too fast to register. A hotel high up on a mountain side above the city. On all sides below us houses climbing up, up, up from below, as if in hope they might somehow reach us. A magnificent, seemingly Grand Canyon-wide drop out over the houses and the city to the blue spread of lake below. The snow-peaked alps in the distance beyond. And then we were off to Germany.

To pick up where I left off earlier, not only were Peter Meyer-Dohm and Rita Suessmuth still pushing partnership, but also, we were to discover, so were many others. Riane was again to share the podium with Professor Suessmuth, this time at a beautiful Rathaus in Berlin.

3,000 Years of Love

Known as "the red city hall," one is sometimes told this was the historic site for President John F. Kennedy's famous "Ich bin ein Berliner" speech defying Russia prior to the fall of the Berlin wall. In fact, this was the massive renaissance-style city hall *behind* the Iron Curtain in East Berlin at the time, while Kennedy spoke at another Rathaus in West Berlin. In any case, once inside this Rathaus one is quickly willing to toss history aside and go with the legend. A magnificent red-carpeted staircase leads up to a beautiful chandelier-lit hall with walls that immediately tell you this is a historic place.

In the state room we gathered in, on one wall is a giant mural depicting the fall of the Berlin wall and in the buildings of a sun-washed new city the rebirth of the nation. On the other wall is another giant mural of picnics, bathers in streams, lovers, and the gathering of happy families to signal the spirit of the new Germany.

Properly portentous, Peter introduced the event. With a fist-chopping honesty and hearty passion I wish we could again see at the top in American politics, culminating in a stirring and moving paean on the subject of Riane and Riane's work, Rita spoke. With her particular brand of eloquence, Riane then spoke. Then everybody poured out into the hall for the book signing. Amid the milling around, and chatting, we met our German publisher, Lienhardt Valentin, and the organizers for more events.

The first of these was a conference at the famous Berlin School of Economics with the director and teachers in the Harriet Taylor economics program.

This was a fascinating experience for several reasons. One, because of the significance of the decision by the Berlin School of Economics to launch a program honoring Harriet Taylor, the lover and then wife of the great classic economist John Stuart Mill, whom Mill had credited as the co-creator of his key works. Another reason was because of increasing interest in the economic theories of the turn-of-the-century feminist writer, thinker, and activist Charlotte Perkins Gilman—known primarily in America as the writer of "The Yellow Wallpaper," a harrowing short story of a woman going mad in a suffocating male-dominated marriage.

Already well into writing her own new book on *caring* economics, *The Real Wealth of Nations,* Riane spoke briefly of this new book scheduled for publication by Berrett-Kohler in 2007.

The director of the program was a very attractive blonde, sleeves-rolled-up, athletic woman with a direct, no-nonsense delivery for her words and movements. We were joined by Peter, a professor of economics originally, and other faculty and graduate students. With the others gathered in the room chiming in, the two of them and Riane for a good bit of time exchanged views on how the traditionally male field of economics could be advanced in the directions Riane was exploring. Essentially what they were tackling was how economics could be expanded beyond the presently prevailing dominator model base into the kind of partnership model-oriented economics that supports, rather than inhibits or undermines, the nurturance and caring needed to build a world of peace and a more just sharing of prosperity for all.

All in all, because of the very existence of this program within one of the most prestigious business schools in Europe, this seemed to me a meaningful exchange and potential advance for the women's movement.

We next moved on to a gathering of spiritual activists. Here the three of us—Riane, Peter, and I—found ourselves in the interesting role of guru. On the floor on all sides around us were seated those with questions seeking our wisdom.

Aside from connecting with the remarkable Rita Suessmuth once again in the Rathaus, the high point, however, was going with Peter again to Wolfsburg. We had the boost of finding the International Partnership Initiative that Goudevert and Peter had launched still functioning, with an office and staff for Peter and programs still actively advancing the partnership ethos in many areas of Germany. Then that night we gathered with Peter and Uta and a number of bright and charming folk for a party in their home.

Women, men, some young and bright-eyed, some ancient and grey, all exuding an unusual consideration for one another, these were the faithful participants who weekly and monthly, year after year since we had originally been there, had gathered with Peter and Uta to explore and advance the partnership way of feeling, thinking, and acting.

It was a moving experience.

And so it has been. Even in face of a global regression to the domination model, the push toward partnership goes on. Every year Riane is invited to keynote major conferences in Europe, Latin America, Canada, and the United States. During recent years she spoke in Colombia, invited by the Mayor of Bogota. In the Czech Republic, invited by Vaclav Havel, then president. At the opening plenary for the Barcelona Women's Forum on 2004. In Argentina, to 4,000 educators from all over Latin America. She's also spoken at scores of business conferences, at corporations ranging from Du Pont, Disney, and Arthur Anderson to Microsoft and Sidley, Austin, Brown, and Wood. The universities where she's spoken range from Yale, Haverford, Goddard College, Case Western Reserve and UCLA to the University of St.

Gallen, the University of Costa Rica, the University of Helsinki, and the University of Bologna.

She remains President of the Center for Partnership Studies (www.partnershipway.org) and actively involved in the Spiritual Alliance to Stop Intimate Violence (www.saiv.net), which she co-founded. She also founded the Alliance for a Caring Economy. She's received many honors, from the Humanist Pioneer Award to membership in the World Council for Global Consciousness and Spirituality. And in 2004, amid the gowned, bannered, capped, and seemingly endless slow march of the faculty and graduates in commencement ceremony, was awarded an honorary doctorate of humanities by Case Western Reserve University.

She's also involved in the Montessori Foundation's Center for Partnership Education with its annual conferences, which like the Goddard University Masters degree in partnership education, is designed to make her work available to educators at all levels. She's been working on prospective films based on her life and work. After she finishes her new book on economics for Berrett-Kohler, she plans to return to the manuscript of still another book advancing her Cultural Transformation and Relational Dynamics theories.

As for me, as much as possible I hide away from all temptations to go anywhere and give talks. Many years ago I was in on the ground floor and offered the same road that took my good friend Frank McGee, who tragically died of cancer back in the Huntley and Brinkley days, to the top at NBC. But I left television news, wisely intuiting I was cut out for private writing, not public speaking.

We will continue to work for a better world as long as we have the strength—and, let us hope, on beyond.

TWENTY-FOUR
MORE POEMS

Thanks to the way the Glacier chills the Flame, we've got used to not only thinking but writing in terms of the separate categories into which our minds have been chopped. Hence, unconsciously, I believe, a feeling of guilt, of a subtle but dangerous transgression, may creep into us whenever we stray beyond the boundaries of customary expectation to collapse things supposed to be kept separate into one another.

This feeling has worked on me here in interjecting poetry into prose. But the urge persists, for in expressing how things were, or are, or can or should be, prose can go just so far and then must stop.

It is like the rental car that takes you over all the miles to the spot where thereafter you can only go by canoe, or by horseback, or by suddenly, miraculously, sprouting wings. It makes it possible for you to go on beyond the "No Trespassing Sign" to gather the kindling and the firewood for the campfire in the woods, and to sit there in the night looking into the coals and the flames, thinking and talking of the things of the heart as well as mind.

David Loye

If I Could Have a Wish

If I could have a wish today
it would be that I could pick a bouquet
for you that might live forever.
And you to look upon the fresh
faces of those flowers with eternal
delight, with them there forever.
And I likewise to look upon you
as centuries gave way to aeons, and
the aeons became a tunnel, and
then a great tendril that reaches out
through time to become again a flower
in an everlasting garden.

If I could have a second wish,
it would be for you simply to look up at me,
now, this instant, and smile upon me with
love meeting the love in my eyes.

That, too, would open the gate and
passage through the roses to eternity.

3,000 Years of Love

There is this Force Field Healers Say

There is this force field healers say
they are attuned to, some say it comes
from God, others say they do not know, it
is just there. Through them it seems to
pour into, or surround, or bathe those they
heal with an unseen but tangible light.
It is love, they say, the force of love.
Others report suddenly being transported
to a great height from which they can
see the world, indeed the universe, in
glory beyond describing. There is again
involved this force of love, they say.
Or it comes upon us as an enormous
expansion of one's self, of one's
consciousness expanding to embrace all
life, everywhere, in caring intimacy.
Or it is what so softly, quietly explodes
within us looking into the heart of a flower
of a certain color on those mornings when
everything about us, weightless, air born,
ascending, dances in a different light.
It comes to us looking at our child asleep.
It comes to us when hearing an old song.
It comes to us seeing nobility walk among us.

(continued)

David Loye

There it is again when, weary beyond
endurance, we give up and give ourselves
over to whatever remains, down beneath it
all, eternally there, when all else is gone.
Oh look to the sky, the trees, the finger of
cloud just touching the moon! Look up and
see the high touch and the working wings of
that tiny bird for which I have no name!

All this is love, all these are its voices,
all this as in a mighty swirl of energies
seen and unseen is this force that has its
tides, its waves, winds, storms, calm days,
quiet nights, the call and deep sounding of
earth's choir, and all the times of eye, heart,
mind and soul widening magic like the sea.

Oh yes, I know and you know all this so well!
It is what caught the two of us up as leaves
in the playful arms of the wind that from long
ages ago knew us, was looking for us; that knew
the time had come that day, and the night
thereafter, that our lives began.

3,000 Years of Love

All We Have Shared

All we have shared, it comes back
to me now, like the sunset flung out
in a scarlet scarf across the western sky
then violet waning over the sea
out from Carmel; but also like the sunrise
exploding out of the Great Rift Valley,
and the plane rising like the eye of
God or Goddess looking down on the
ancient land of one's creation.

The midnight walk wild and hand in hand
ecstatic, reveling in the Parisian chatter and
the glitter of the Champs-Elysees.

The rumble of the hoofs, the earth shakes
and down into the river surge the wildebeast
to struggle up on our side to stream on past
us, a million on the move.

The jeep with the proud black driver shooting
through the shoulder high sea of grass.

And spring, and the walk through the woods
near Wolfsburg, the earth rich and moist, the
fresh smells of pine and flowers, the green of green
and the gold of gold in the touch of sunlight filtering
through the new young leaves.

(continued)

David Loye

And Ravello, high there above the fairyland
towers and domes and laddered streets of
the old world wonder of Amalfi—to stand there
together on the statued balcony and look out over
the sparkling blue spread of the Mediterranean on
and on and on.

And Crete, and the magic of Knossos and Gournia
speaking over millennia to us, supposedly dead and
gone but spiritually as alive, and as immortal, as we
ourselves.

The Sunset Canyon pool, and you lying there on
the grass in your blue bathing suit beneath the
sycamore trees, and me raised up on an elbow
gazing upon you, and all the wonder in our hopes
so vast they could not possibly ever be realized—
and to find them surpassed now every day.

And so I read to you in bed at night,
and we are side by side there glorying
in this mate, this pal, this rare presence
always there even when you or I
travel alone.

And it seems the best of all,
but all and so much more is the
best of life we've shared.

It is good.
It is the way it should be.

TWENTY-FIVE
GOODBYE SOMETIME

A few years ago I dictated most of these memories to a tape recorder, for transcription by our household savior and Director of CPS Operations, Leah Gowron, while I was bed-ridden for nearly two months. It was the second time around for recovering from an operation for a detached retina in the eye.

It had happened a year earlier leaving me with a weird, diminished, chopped up and cross-hatched world out of that eye. Now it had happened again with my good eye.

This kind of operation forces one to lie face down on one's stomach for at least two weeks, and then if the healing is progressing well, to further lie around without reading or doing anything else that might jar loose the lightly reattached retina before it has had time to securely heal in place. This had forced me to shut down writing all the books that kept pressing to get out of me.

It had forced me to simply lie there, or sit and feel around me the presence of all that each day in a hurry to get on with it, whatever it was, I rushed by—ah so often, for all of us too often, barely seeing or feeling the ever-emergent glory of this earth. So seldom appreciating it. So seldom giving thanks for this most precious gift of all. It forced me to lie there and think back on the good years Riane and I have had together, roaming out from and then returning to this beloved home place.

And so now again in mind I sit here in the kitchen and fondly stroke the polished surface of the granite breakfast table. Only a few years ago the remodeling of this kitchen was completed after a year of frustration in which I was forced to cook our meals on a hot plate in my office in the studio outside.

Now here it is, the realization of Riane's dream of a new kitchen that might evoke the magic of ancient Minoan Crete. The polished granite countertops and breakfast table, along with the extension into what had been the old pantry, were cut to fit the odd angles of this arrangement from the giant slab of granite we located after a long search. It appealed to us as it seems a match for the coloring and patterning of the background for murals on the island of Santorini, where the best of the Minoan murals were found.

Inset into the tiles of the splash board ringing the countertops and circling the room is a Minoan pattern of blue byzantine waves composed of tiny bits of stone mosaic. Overheard, to either side of the skylight flooding this kitchen and giving it that warm sense of the Mediterranean, are the beams carefully tinted by a specialty painter along the fluted side edges with alternating strips of the salmon red and crystalline blue characteristic of Minoan art.

I walk, and for the first time in some time I realize how much I love the look of the long galleria from the dining room down to the bedroom end of the house.

On one side is a row of windows pouring in light from the North. On the other side are two laden bookshelves, and between them a red and yellow Kilim wedding rug hangs from the high ceiling to the floor.

Down the hall is the long golden runner underfoot—this rug mellowed in just the right way with age, along with its companion for the

3,000 Years of Love

hall that angles off towards the bedrooms.

Moving into the living room, for the first time in a long time I marvel at the giant rug that fills the room from end to end and wall to wall, along with the long runners in the halls, all this mellow golden expanse of rug custom-woven in China many years ago for a former owner to exactly fit this house.

Catching the light that pours into the living room from the great multi-paned window from the south, this aged rug has the look of a distant wheat field at harvest time I can remember from those days when I was sixteen working the harvest in Minnesota. I sit here in this special room in "my" chair by the lamp and quietly bask in the sense of a friendly unseen larger living presence the room gives one.

It is a room that seems to say "sit down, relax, and just be, all is well."

And what do the floor to ceiling shelves laden with our books on either side of the large casement window say?

"Relax. Enjoy. For here with no longer the need to read them you can savor the presence of the treasures of millions of lives, and thousands of minds, over hundreds of years, all stored here for you any time you may want to dip into them again."

The wood paneling and general look to the room is of an old English house or the posh club rooms at Princeton, where long ago I once taught. The massive fireplace mantle is set off at either end by the two large silver candelabra of elegant Austrian Empire design, part of the few possessions Riane's parents carried with them when they fled the Nazis.

Across from me is the long divan of a pleasing, clean line in a soft velvet of a salmon shade, almost voluptuous in tone, long enough to lie down on. Or for four or five guests. Or children and grand children to sit side-by-side. Or for that rare gathering of friends for my 80th birthday party, when my treasured soul brother the world-wandering "children's troubadour" Raffi flew down from Vancouver to sing Beatle songs and his own deeply moving "Salaam, Shalom." And for Nelson Mandela, "Turn This World Around." And dedicated to Riane, "Tomorrow's Children"—with the haunting line "If not for wonder, if not for reverence, If not for love, why have we come here?"

Sitting here, in mind watching Raffi swaying, weaving, dancing, grinning, once again I hear him singing

> Tomorrow's children stand in the garden
> They stand at twilight in every nation
> Their eyes are on you, they're not mistaken
> Tomorrow's children are not for sale
>
> Tomorrow's children play in the forest
> Their eyes are clear, they look for kindness
> Arm in arm, they need no logo,
> Tomorrow's children, not for sale.
>
> Tomorrow's young dance in the doorway
> Circle songs stream down the hallway
> We know their cries, we know their laughter
> Tomorrow's promise whispering today
>
> Tomorrow's children, reading Eisler
> Planting seeds along the harbour
> Closing ranks to save the shoreline
> Tomorrow's children lead the way

3,000 Years of Love

If not for wonder, if not for reverence
If not for love, why have we come here?
Tomorrow's young now at daybreak
Learning how to heal the heartache

Tomorrow's children, brilliant poppies
Of every hue and inspiration
Just in time for our salvation
Tomorrow's children lead the way

© 2002 Homeland Publishing

Once again I am watching the angle and flash of Raffi's fingers over the frets of his guitar. Again I hear the sudden startling bell tones of the harmonics that he throws in, all to resonate with the childhood soul I should say of all those who were gathered here then, to reverberate within the hallowed chamber of this room.

Between my chair and the divan is the glass coffee table with its stack of art books at either end and vase holding one of Riane's striking arrangements of flowers from our garden.

This is one of her great pleasures—to weekly move through the garden to select and then cut and shape the bundled touches of roses, geraniums, camelias, Peruvian lilies, and lilies-of-the-Nile that in strategic places dot the house with these varied bursts of color. They seem to say, "be joyful, for there is beauty in even the darkest corners of our world."

And so I sit here facing the glass table and the divan, in one of the two massive, squared-off chairs of modern Spanish design—each slightly angled toward the table and the divan, to invite an intimacy of those gathered around the table to talk and get to know one another and share ideas.

Overhead the massive beams across the ceiling seem to say, "the sky may fall elsewhere, but never here."

And at the other end of the room, toward the glassed-in patio, sits the massive and majestic falcon of polished red clay of Tonela artistry.

I found it myself in that crafts-persons village in Mexico, Tonela. And I revel in the fact I bought it for only ten dollars, and wouldn't part with it for thousands.

Walking now outside in my mind's eye, I look at the giant oak that is our garden's most formidable piece of living sculpture.

It is one of the grove of thirty or so California live oaks, lush with leaves year-round, which ring our house and garden with their druid embrace. This one, however, is the grandfather, or grandmother, or Shaman and Shamaness of them all, its gnarled and curling branches angling off in all directions eighty feet into the air, and eighty feet from side-to-side.

It is like those figures of sinuous body and many arms and legs, of the Hindu goddesses Devi, Durga, Kali, Lakshmi, Sarasvati, and Shakti transformed from stone into a tree, as if caught here in a stop-motion photograph of an ancient dance of benign incantation.

Down the graveled path now in mind I go, past the lemon tree and the Japanese cherry, which explodes into its mass of delicate pink blossoms each spring. And the two-tiered field of African daisies is now before me, awash in a sea of purple, white, and green. And there above the higher tier, up the brick steps and pathway set off by the roses and the boxed hedges, is the house from the outside.

3,000 Years of Love

I see in mind that massive, iron-clasped wooden door. And the neat sprawl and Mediterranean look to the stucco of the massive white walls and red-brown shake roof, with the two white chimneys standing on guard against the blue of a clean and pure sky.

Down there beyond the trees stands the high white cinder block wall surrounding this acre of wonderment, with the largest gate allowing cars into our inner parking area, screened off from the house and gardens by a double-gated inner wall.

It is in every sense that matters, physically, emotionally, intellectually, and spiritually, a sanctuary.

It is this place she sees and delights in every day, for she has the rare and enduring, ever-renewing, capacity for a child's delight, and this in so many ways is her creation.

> "Tomorrow let's go again,
> while the earth is wet."
> This you said to me last
> night after we had spent our
> third day gardening together.
>
> What a simple thing, yet
> how profoundly important!
> To get out of our separate
> driven heads, alternating
> between the ecstasy of scaling
> the mightiest of mountains
> and despair over whether
> an ounce of this will ever
> matter, and just be together.

(continued)

David Loye

"Tomorrow, let's go again,
while the earth is wet."

Yes, let's go again, and
then again, to wherever
life is simple, real, and
restorative.

After all, what is it that
in the end will matter?
Only that we found each
other, and shared these
years.

The years pass but not our love.
Like the evergreen of the great
live oaks, the year-round green
and gold of gazanias, the soft
orange red of the impatiens nodding

in their pots...like the ever-
returning fragrance of the roses,
the gentle touch of orange and lemon
blossoms on the wind, the bold showers
of camelias, and the dance of poppies
and daisies everywhere,
it is eternal.

Lost in all the projects in my head, I realize how little of this I am normally aware of. I begin to see and fully appreciate the special meaning we have implanted into the trees and walks and walls of this one small place, leaving it briefly to roam the Earth to come to know and value people elsewhere, but always returning here for renewal.

I think of old Mrs. Parsons next door of the sparkling eye and wit, who in her nineties was still going strong, but alas now is gone. I think of how she and I both enjoyed kidding and joshing and gossiping with one another over the wall or in the supermarket, when we met, as neighbors in the "old times" used to do.

I think of the beautiful red fox, who for several weeks at a time would lie on the white gravel of the small courtyard and garden just outside the windows to our bedroom and Riane's office. We tiptoed around to keep from disturbing her, and for most of a year she or he came and went. And of the tiny flock of acorn woodpeckers who occasionally suddenly appear to flutter and whisper among our oaks.

A rare species, they live in only two places on this Earth. One place is way out in Carmel Valley within the protection of the Hastings Research Sanctuary. Considering what we are trying to promote among our own difficult species, quite fittingly these acorn woodpeckers are one of the most striking instances of a "partnership society" in the bird world. They forage for and store acorns for community consumption, look after one another's offspring, and do other thoughtful things for one another. They come all the way in from Hastings to harvest our acorns apparently when the pickings are slim out there.

I think of the crows who occasionally have a convention in our trees. And the perky, pesky, highly intelligent California Jays, cousin to the common American Blue Jay, this nervous high-energy bird that darts about in search of the careless bug and decries the invasion of the occasional neighborhood cat. The raccoons who used to hold wild

David Loye

parties at night on top of the roof to my office, but who seem now to have gone elsewhere. I think, too, of their little stone companions, the rabbit and the frog, side-by-side in our unfortunately rather woebegone and neglected succulent garden.

> Like an old, old friend,
> time and me go way back when.
> And I know now
> what I didn't know then.
> I wish I could start all over again.

The lines are from a song by Tom Paxton, who writes and sings songs of which Riane and I are fond.

Tom, who I wish I knew but don't, is a fellow Oklahoman, from Tulsa, big city neighbor to Bartlesville, where I grew up. I used to play the guitar and sing songs myself, with a voice friends say reminds them of Tom's. At eighty-one, I can still sing almost as well as ever. Riane, radiant and beautiful at seventy-five, still passes for someone twenty years younger.

We have a ways to go yet, of this I am sure. But we have entered that time when it feels good to think of and as much as possible be with our separately-generated children and grandchildren, and to think and with love remember all the friends we have known along the way.

I think also of those who have been our brain children and grandchildren, all the books and ideas born not of the blood but out of mind together. Many we have known of those who will live beyond us, in particular moved by Riane's books. But many more we shall never know personally, but out of our books, thoughts, and what we aspired to they will know us.

3,000 Years of Love

They will come to know that what counts to people who have set out to try to change our world in any way for the better is the hope they might make some lasting difference somewhere.

> Oh world that carries us in this wondrous
> womb in time! Can you sense our gratitude?
> Can you hasten the time of the gathering of
> all of us here on the high plateau, with the
> night of love going on forever, and the day
> an endless song?

Ours may be, or may not be a lasting difference—one can hope, but what matters is that we've tried.

These days, the exciting young people of a new generation are beginning to come into our lives. Not too long ago there came here to film us, for a documentary they were making, three young men who I think will make it over the long run. Self-financed, living on a budget of hamburgers and as much as possible free overnights in the homes of friends along the way, driven by ambition but even more so by the old urge of recording some of the fascination and wonder of the activist mind, they were roaming the country interviewing people like us for a DVD to be called "Utopia." Out of what has become by now thousands of feet of high quality digital recording, they want to craft something to capture the fire of the vision of America and of the world at its best.

Seeing now in mind the nervous flutter of thousands of oak moths that had taken over our place at the time they filmed us, I see their project and hundreds, and one can hope thousands more like it, as doing something desperately needed in the bland, blind and increasingly so dreadfully dangerous delusion of our time.

David Loye

I think of the beautiful Jules Hart behind her camera, the former model and actress, and of the incredibly talented artist John Mason, among all of those who have pulled together crews to capture Riane on film. Of Patrick O'Heffernan, the Emmy-winning producer, and of Timothy Karsten and the gorgeous Karinna Kittles, who've set out to try to pull all the film and tapes and CDs into the programs or documentaries her life and works calls for. And of Martin Rausch and Claus Biegert, whose documentary on peace uses Riane's work on Partnership and Domination as its framework.

Within the dominator detour of our lost time, I like to think that what the new camera activists of this and all other nations come up with may sear through the pudding of television like a hot iron, and help jolt the minds we must reach back on track to the ancient promised land.

And so it goes.
Summer and fall give way to winter and then spring.
The leaves of the tree become the nutrient that drives up through the roots and trunk to again become the leaves and flowers and fruit.
The fiery orb of the sun sinks into the endlessly vast, gleaming and rolling spread of water out from the beach as together we walk beside the ocean. Like stately galleons, a flight of pelicans crosses the glory of the afterglow.
Gently the night settles in, our earth revolves in space, the Milky Way inches a bit along its trajectory out there within the embrace of our galaxy of planets and stars. And then, with morning, there is the sun again rising to gild the green of the oaks and the pines with the rose gold light of a new day.
Here's to our children, and grandchildren, and all the friends we

3,000 Years of Love

have known and wished we could have spent more time with, and our readers over the past years and for years to come. Here's to you.

TWENTY-SIX
3,000 YEARS OF LOVE

The thought that death will part us forever is too much to bear. We do not want to believe it. I do not believe it.

Perhaps my faith is only fantasy. Perhaps it's real. No one knows.

Will we be together again? Have we been together before?

Locked into the here and now that most of the time grips us, I had routinely fixed the date when Riane and I met as January 22, 1977. But then something happened that led me to wonder whether it wasn't a good deal earlier.

Somewhere around 3,000 years earlier, as a matter of fact.

Which, in turn, opens up the question, could it actually have been even earlier?

Through my interest as a psychologist in exploring as much of the "new" territory in consciousness studies as I could find time for, I had come up against the question raised by the approach widely known today as "past life regression."

When we just read about it, it rather quickly bumps up against our natural skepticism, however open-minded we try to be. But when you go through it, your perception of the world, and who you are within it, can be radically changed.

3,000 Years of Love

Here's what happened to me.

As we had found worked in the course of several explorations, I was told by my fellow psychologist and friend Nadya Giusi to go ahead and put myself in a trance. Normally a light hypnotic trance is induced by the person you are working with, but as I was practiced in self-hypnosis, it was quicker this way. I could do it with just three deep breaths, and then I was in the aptly called "altered state of consciousness."

In one way of looking at it, little has changed. You are perfectly aware at all times of yourself and every detail of your present surroundings. But it is as though you are standing slightly to one side of it all looking in.

"Where are you this time?" Nadya asks.

I had expected some strange and unfamiliar setting, as in previous explorations. The first time I was ostensibly living in the ice age, 10,000 years ago. In a particularly rich journey that I later investigated with startling results—of which I write in *Return to Amalfi*—I was a spice merchant in the year 1611 in that delightful spot in Italy, of which I had no knowledge at the time. But this time there was something awfully familiar about the place.

Spread out on the flattened top of a hill, it seemed to be a palace of sorts. Flat roofed. Bright red supporting columns. Something like a row of stone abstractions of bull's horns running along its roof line. A sense of olive trees somewhere in the greenery of a distant hill.

With a shock I recognized it. This was the "palace" of Knossos in Minoan Crete. Intact and new. Which meant I was supposedly back in time over 3,000 years. It would have been around 1400 B.C., before it was destroyed by the first of the two great earthquakes that hit around then, decimating this great early island civilization.

My first reaction was of course that I was undoubtedly making it up this time because I had visited Minoan Crete and had since then also seen the palace in pictures many times. Moreover, as we've seen, the Minoan culture, was especially meaningful to me because of *The Chalice and the Blade*, in which it plays such a key part.

I decided, however, to play along with the emerging picture to see where this would go.

"Look down. What do you see? What are you wearing?"

This was standard procedure, as for some reason looking down at your feet seems to best ground one in wherever one supposedly is and whenever the supposed time may be.

"I see some kind of sandals. Moving up along my legs, they are bare, very muscular and hairy. I seem to be wearing some kind of smock —."

I paused with a chuckle.

"What is it?"

"I don't look at all like I would have thought I'd look."

"What do you mean?"

"I mean all the men in pictures of Minoan Crete are slim, wasp-waisted, clean-shaven, and rather feminine in appearance. I am a stocky, barrel-chested guy with a curly beard, not at all like what I am supposed to look like."

"Where did you come from originally?" Nadya asks.

"I was on an island. It wasn't Crete. Smaller. I was bored and yearned to go to sea. When I was ten I left it, I would guess as some kind of cabin boy."

From this point on, in answer to questions by Nadya designed to prompt each change of scene, the story emerged that I was a sailor in the

3,000 Years of Love

Minoan merchant fleet, actually second in command on my ship.

"Where do you live? What does your house look like?"

This truly startled me. It was at the end of a long ramp or heavy bridge spanning the green gulley between the high plateau on which the palace stood to the town on the opposite hillside. It was a specific house with a slanted peaked roof over a floor of packed earth or clay, rimmed with a seating area that dipped into a well of sorts.

In other words, running around the room next to the wall, at floor level, was what amounted to a bench upon which you and your guests could sit at your leisure to eat and talk. Your feet rested on the lower floor level of the "well," upon which you walked to get around the room, or to reach another room or rooms of some sort farther back.

"What is of special interest in this life?"

Immediately there appeared this beautiful girl, her features indistinct. I only knew she was incredibly beautiful, that I was in love with her, and she with me, and that our life together, although complicated, was wonderful.

The complication, it turned out, was that she was a young priestess in training at the palace. Her life, by tradition, was to be devoted to the worship of the Goddess and the rituals for providing the rest of us ordinary folk with access to the love and the bounty of this higher being.

Contrary to the custom for nuns or priests in our day, neither she nor any of the other priestesses in training were celibate. Sex was accepted as both a devotional and pleasurable thing, so we enjoyed a delightful sex life. Sometimes she would visit me in my house, sometimes I was with her in the palace. The only thing about it was the understanding this could lead to nothing formally permanent in the sense of a marriage. It must remain secondary to her service to the Goddess.

We moved easily in and out of the gatherings and parties of the palace social life, enjoying the status of "that beautiful young couple" until our first crisis. She had become pregnant. She wanted to have the child. I dreaded the thought. It would change, and I felt even might possibly destroy our life together.

I loved the life at sea—the storms, the trading from port to port, the danger of attack by pirates, having good men under my command. To become a land-locked father with some dreary land-bound job was the last thing on earth I wanted.

In the end she had a miscarriage. And for the first time in experiencing this supposed past life, I suddenly had a sharp sense of the possibility of its reality, rather than its being something I was just making up. For the relief I felt was so real—I was very much there, feeling such a complex play of emotion. Feeling her mix of agony, despair, and guilt over the loss, feeling it as mine. But at the same time, most of all, feeling this great, load-lifting and soaring sigh from within of relief, of freedom as though after facing slavery.

"What was the most important event in your life?"

Instantly, I was there as the earth shook and in the town all life stopped for us in the first wave of concern. We were used to recurrent tremors, this happened frequently, but from the first this had the feeling of something worse.

I was in my house. I started for the door and just as I emerged the first great shock hit, I was thrown to the ground, and the house collapsed behind me. I struggled up to see the town crumbling all about me. My first thought was who can I rescue, but in the chaos of the aftershock and all that destruction it was impossible to know where to begin.

The sky was red as I had never seen it before. The whole sky flame red and filled with something I could only identify later as chunks of rock and ashes. Had there been a fire? No fire could be that big.

Then the second great shock hit and as again I rose from the ground to which I had been hurled, looking out toward the palace complex on the hill across from us, I saw the great bridge connecting the town to the palace crumble and go down. Then, to my horror, I saw the palace itself begin to crumble and go down.

No, no—she was there, it mustn't be. I tore down through the rubble to the bottom of the little valley and then fought my way up the hillside to the palace complex.

Amid the ruins the living were still in shock, some wandering wide-eyed in the open where buildings had been before, others already tearing at the stones to try to rescue those who had been buried.

I ran from one group to another asking whether anyone had seen her. No one had.

I knew here and now, in this life—or felt, or in keeping maybe with a desire to find some meaning in this catastrophe now supposedly thousands of years later believed—that the young priestess was Riane.

Yes, yes of course it was her. Given an ounce of meaning to life beyond what we can only briefly glimpse during our few, short years on this earth, who else could it have been?

I worked through the day and into the next day with everyone else, pulling apart the stones and fallen timbers. I did this in part still looking for her. But in part I knew for sure she was dead and I was simply trying to help the others.

In the end, responding to the insistence of my sense of responsibility to the only meaningful thing I had left, I returned to my ship amid the wreckage of our fleet in the harbor to see if it could be put back in shape to resume trading.

Here in Nadya's office, my chest was heaving, I was gasping, and the sense of loss was overwhelming.

"Do you want to stop?" Nadya asked in concern.

I shook my head.

"Maybe you should lie down and rest for a minute," she said.

I nodded and did so, then nodded again when I felt ready to go on.

"Let's advance to the day of your death. What happens?"

I am on my ship in the middle of a storm. I am surprised to find that I am wearing a sort of armored breastplate—which makes no sense, but there is no time to wonder why as the experience unfolds so rapidly I must race in mind to keep up with it.

The wind is so intense and the waves are so high, the ship shuddering as it sinks into the trough between waves, the flood across the deck carrying some of us overboard, we know we can easily be swamped and sunk. But what I remember so distinctly is how confident I felt.

Somehow I knew I was invincible. I would survive—and then the boom for a sail that had been torn away came sweeping across the deck, caught me in the neck, and instantly killed me.

Had this really happened? To this day I waver between belief and disbelief.

For a number of reasons I find the question difficult to resolve one way or the other.

First there was the earthquake. I had known beforehand of the well-documented fact that an earthquake had accompanied the cataclysmic explosion of the volcano that blew the lid off the nearby island of Thera, or Santorini as it's known today. I had known this shattered the palace complex on Crete and rained down debris and ashes for days afterward. But on checking sources carefully I found there had been not one but two of these great earthquakes. The two were fifty years apart, and what I supposedly had experienced was closer to what happened after the second and most devastating rather than the first earthquake.

Next was the discrepancy in how I looked—not at all like all the customary pictures of slim, wasp-waisted Minoan men. Then one day I came across this reference to the sailors of that ancient time and place attributed to Plato.

"The sailors of Minos were from Caria."

Caria? Where was Caria? I found that it was an ancient land located on the mainland where Turkey is today. Then I realize this was where the bloody nation of Assyria was located in earlier ancient times. And in the stiff, fierce pictures of what Assyrian men looked like there was, indeed, my body type!

The same curly black hair, curly black beard. The same stocky body, with chest, arms and legs in which the muscles stood out like the taut stretch of steel cables.

Checking further I found that Caria extended out into a series of small islands off the coast that like a wavering arrow pointed on out toward Crete.

There was the giant Assyria in ancient times, and above it tiny Caria, and Caria spread out into the islands—among which could have been the island I had supposedly left at age ten. So this seemed to account for how I became a sailor in the Cretan merchant fleet.

Next was my house. It just didn't look anything like the pictures of houses in Minoan Crete, which were flat roofed, not peaked as I had seen. But some years later when Riane and I accompanied the great archeologist Marija Gimbutas on a trip to one of her "digs" in northern Greece, I was amazed to see an exact reconstruction of "my house" in a model that showed what the houses of the prehistoric village Gimbutas had excavated looked like. The peaked roof of straw or sticks. Even the same "living room," with the ground level bench around the periphery of the room and with pit for feet.

I told Marija of the coincidence and my difficulty with my house in Knossos.

"This is of course northern Greece," I said. "But could there possibly have been such a house so far south from here, also in Minoan Crete?"

"Of course," she said. "I have no doubt of it."

Then there was what I was wearing when killed in the storm. If the Minoans were such a remarkably peaceful people, how could I have been wearing an armored breast plate?

When I thought about that, I realized that one of the reasons for the evidence of a remarkable state of peace over hundreds of years for this island culture was probably that the Minoans had the reputation for crafting the best swords of their time and in the arming of their merchant vessels against pirates had the most effective navy for the Mediterranean. I also was thunderstruck some years later to find a picture of exactly the kind of breast plate I had worn identified in a research volume as "Cretan breastplate."

It was identified as ninth century B.C., which would have been off by 500 years. But that's ninth century *B.C.,* before Christ, back when technology changed at a snail's pace, not ninth century *A.D*, as change began to speed up. And as favorite designs are passed on from generation to generation, could this not have been a replica of what

3,000 Years of Love

existed earlier?

There was also this about the bridge between the village where I lived and the "palace" on the other side of the dip of the valley between us. At the time of my past-life regression, I had absolutely no knowledge that such a bridge had ever existed. It was only after this strange probe into the possible past that I discovered a striking picture of just such a bridge, as reconstructed by artists from the analysis of accounts and fragments by archeologists.

Finally—least believable to anyone who hasn't personally experienced something like this, but most haunting to me in retrospect—was what happened when I again visited the palace complex in Crete after the earlier regression experience.

I was with a chattering group with a guide. But wanting to see if I might somehow reconnect with that time I held back, and then left the group to stand alone by myself where the bridge would have been.

Looking across the little valley to where the bridge would have ended in the village, to where my house would have been, for a bit I felt nothing. But then it came sweeping over me, and the enormity of that ostensible day 3,000 years ago seized me again.

That horrible sense of loss. Not just for her, but even more for all that this island culture back in time revealed of what life could have been for all of us today, had not for 5,000 years, again and again, the Glacier snuffed out the Flame.

EPILOGUE

So I close this book of the memories of our earliest days and the episodes and thoughts that dot the past and in their interconnection reflect the story of our lives.

I close the book, but not the mind. For of course all this is what comes back to us now, along with all we came to feel, and think, and know, and do together afterward.

All this, and much, much more.

All the joys and all the sorrows that make up life. All that is good and all that is bad. All that matters and does not matter. All the questions that are answered—and the great long abiding mystery that expands out beyond the range of our minds in this lifetime into the eternal question of eternal light or eternal darkness.

Will there be time for us to share our love here on Earth for years still to come?

And when we are gone, will our work matter or last? Will what burned within us take fire in the hearts and minds of others reading of these days and years?

So one hopes.

So I believe—and tried to capture the thought, but more so the feelings, in these two poems I wrote in my seventies while she was still a youngster in her sixties.

3,000 Years of Love

Let There Be Time

Let there be time.
Time for more and more.
Time for your walk among the flowers, clipping,
    clipping, and the basket full, and so to me to
    strip the leaves, and back to you and the magic
    of your arrangements for the big vases, and the
    little vases for the placing of their soft explosions
    of delight throughout the house.

Time for the walk beside the sea on bright days,
    and on grey days, with the birds like quiet
    exclamation points in flight, and west the great
    swell of the ocean going on and on into what our
    hearts seek as infinity.

Time for the comfort, beyond expression, of feeling
    this being more dear to oneself than oneself
    warm beneath the covers beside one.

Time to laugh together, as wild as monkeys, and
    time to weep together when one must.

Time to rage together at the stupidity and the
    insanity.

Time to explore the secret chambers and together
    scale the highest mountains of the mind.

Time for love on and on and on.

David Loye

The Continents Rise and Clash

The continents rise and clash and
split apart, yet love remains.

Trees, flowers, grass, the very
soil beneath our feet is caught up
by the wind, yet love remains.

The flood of mail, magazines, and
messages crests, machines ring out
one last time, yet love remains.

I look at you, you look at me, our
eyes meeting melt into a single
golden crystal through all eternity,
and love remains.

For further information on books by Riane Eisler, see www.rianeeisler.com and the website for the Center for Partnership Studies, www.partnershipway.org.

For further information on books by David Loye, see the websites for The Benjamin Franklin Press, www.benjaminfranklinpress.com; for The Darwin Project, www.thedarwinproject.com.; and eventually www.davidloye.com.

ABOUT OUR COVER

Our cover is an original painting by the noted American artist Barbara Schaefer, with the fascinating overlay effect for the cover by the noted American artist John Mason.

This cover painting is from a small book handmade by Barbara Schaefer containing a spectacular set of such small paintings that Schaefer gave to author Riane Eisler to celebrate Eisler's book *The Chalice and the Blade.*

Other paintings from this unique personal treasure and museum piece have been used by Mason for the covers for books of Loye's poems referred to in this book, *1001 Days of Love* and *100 Days of Love.*

Barbara Schaefer's studio is in New York City. You can see more of her striking paintings on her website: www.barbaraschaeferart.com.

ABOUT THE AUTHOR

Behind the books of David Loye lies an unusual career path. While a very young news correspondent with the U.S. Navy in the closing years of World War II, he docked and roamed the same ports in South America that Charles Darwin, as a similarly very young man, visited one hundred years earlier on the famous voyage of the Beagle. He became a television newsman during the Edward R. Murrow days. He wrote the national award-winning *The Healing of a Nation* and gained his doctorate in psychology in early middle age. While a Princeton and UCLA School of Medicine faculty member, he was the research director for major studies of political values, the use of the brain and mind in prediction, and the impact of movies and television on adults.

For the past twenty years he has been mainly involved with other scientists from around the world in development of the new fields of evolutionary systems science, chaos and complexity theory, and in studies of Darwin's life and works from these advanced new scientific perspectives. He is a co-founder of two international organizations for advanced evolution studies; a co-founder with his wife and partner—evolution theorist and well-known author of *The Chalice and the Blade,* Riane Eisler—of The Center for Partnership Studies; and founder of The Darwin Project (www.thedarwinproject.com), with a Council of more than 50 leading American, European, and Asian scientists, educators, and media activists. Loye is the author of *The Leadership Passion, The Knowable Future, The Sphinx and the Rainbow, An Arrow through Chaos, Darwin's Lost Theory of Love*, and editor of *The Evolutionary Outrider: The Impact of the Human Agent on Evolution,* and *The Great Adventure: Toward a Fully Human Theory of Evolution.* Among publishers for his books are Norton, Wiley, Jossey-Bass, New Science Library, Park Street Press, Bantam Books, Delacorte, Praeger, Adamantine, Gordon & Breach, the State University of New York (SUNY Press), and publishers in Japan, China, Italy, the Netherlands, and three publishers in Germany.

His new six-book Darwin Anniversary cycle is the product of two decades of work with fellow members of the General Evolution Research Group, of which he was a co-founder, and the International Society of Systems Sciences on advanced studies of evolution. His systems scientific reconstruction of the long ignored "rest of Darwin"—and its corroboration by progressive biologists and brain, social and systems scientists—has been hailed by leading scientists and other scholars as a major contribution to our understanding of Darwin, evolution, and the challenge facing our species in the 21st century.

This new work—which brings to life a much larger and contradictory Darwin and the work of thousands of scientists building a hopeful and humanistic new expansion for the story and theory of evolution—first gained formal book publication in Germany and China. Then late in 2004, the second largest university press in America, State University Press of New York (SUNY Press), published *The Great*

3,000 Years of Love Adventure: Toward a Fully Human Theory of Evolution.

"In times like these a new worldview often arises at the margins of power, at the periphery of the action unfolding on the main stage," internationally known psychologist Mihaly Csikszentmihalyi writes in the foreword to this book by Loye with chapters by eleven other members of the General Evolution Research Group and The Darwin Project Council.

"The themes introduced by the authors are likely to be among the central ones of any new world-view...The organizing principle of the new faith—a faith of human beings about human beings—is evolution itself. Not the traditionally taught evolutionary scenario dominated by competition and selfishness, but an understanding closer to the original Darwinian one that sees cooperation and transcendence of the self as the most exciting parts of the story."

This is the story and the science that Loye unfolds in the six books of the Darwin Anniversary Book Cycle for the Benjamin Franklin Press (www.benjaminfranklinpress.com): *Bankrolling Evolution, Measuring Evolution, Darwin's Lost Theory, Darwin on Love, The Derailing of Evolution,* and *Telling the New Story.*

Additionally, out of the incomplete works in progress of a lifetime, are these other books by Loye being published by Benjamin Franklin Press. Unusual in their range from pioneering in science to tales of adventure, travel, mystery, humor, and love are a Moral Evolution Book Cycle: *The Parable of the Three Villages, The River and the Star, The Glacier and the Flame I, The Glacier and the Flame II,* and *The Science of Evil.* An Entertainment and Humor Book Cycle: *Brave Laughter,*

David Loye

Return to Amalfi, Tangled Tales of the Book Trade or the Mystery of the Missing Century, and *Grandfather's Garden.* And a Love Cycle: *100 Days of Love, 1001 Days of Love,* and *3,000 Years of Love.*

For more on Dr. Loye's books and scientific background, see bios on www.thedarwinproject.com, www.benjaminfranklinpress.com, and www.davidloye.com.

BENJAMIN FRANKLIN PRESS BOOKS 2007-2009
www.benjaminfranklinpress.com

Among our books for 2007-2009 is the unprecedented 22-book creative explosion of new works by the rare partnership of evolutionary scientist-author-activists David Loye, award-winning author of *The Healing of a Nation* and *The Sphinx and the Rainbow,* and Riane Eisler, internationally known author of *The Chalice and the Blade* and *Sacred Pleasure;* Pulitzer nominee political cartoonist and artist Bill Bates, author of the definitive *Bates on Bush* and other classic commentaries.

This announcement is keyed to seasons, holidays, national affairs—in particular the critical 2008 national election. As published, you can find and buy our books from major online book sellers throughout the U.S., Europe, and Asia, or order them through bookstores everywhere.

2007

March, 2007. **National affairs, 2008 election.** Publication of the first two books of the new six-book **Darwin Anniversary Cycle** by David Loye: *Bankrolling Evolution: Money, Politics, and Science,* and *Measuring Evolution: A User's Guide to the Health and Wealth of Nations.* The culmination of thousands of studies by progressive natural and social scientists, this is a revolutionary scientific perspective on how to dig out from the disaster of the

Bush years and get human evolution back on track.

April, 2007. **New Riane Eisler block buster.** Publication of Riane Eisler's *The Real Wealth of Nations: Creating a Caring Economics* by San Francisco publisher Berrett-Kohler. From pre-publication reviews by nearly forty world leaders and celebrities in many fields: " A template for the better world we have been so urgently seeking" ***Nobel Peace Laureate Archbishop Desmond Tutu***. . ."Sure to be a classic." ***Air America radio host Thom Hartman***. . . "Expands the scope and practice of economics beyond capitalism and socialism to a new economics in which equity, justice, and environmental sanity prevail." ***Morris Dees***. . . "What has been desperately needed for a long time." ***Peter Senge***. . ."At a time when we desperately need a new voice for a new kind of economics, this great piece of work arrives, rigorously researched, passionately written, and clear as a bell." ***Lynn Twist***. . ." A call to action." ***Jane Goodall***.

May, 2007. **The perfect summer read.** Publication of the first of six books for an **Entertainment and Humor Cycle** by David Loye, *Brave Laughter* is the inspiring story of three generations of a lake-dwelling Minnesota family of independent thinkers and funny story tellers within the larger picture of change and progressive evolution for America from the Civil War into post-World War II years.

June, 2007. **Travel, adventure, mystery—another perfect summer read.** Publication of the second of Loye's Entertainment and Humor Cycle, *Return to Amalfi*—the real life involvement of Loye and Eisler in a rare combination of travel, detective, romance, history, "ghost," and scientific adventure story.

3,000 Years of Love

***August, 2007.* Romance, adventure, and the rumbling of revolution.** The first of four books with potential for pre-Christmas book sales: Publication of *3,000 Years of Love*—the gripping, inspiring, often funny dual-biography of the lives of Eisler and Loye as lovers, writers, evolutionary systems scientists, and social and political activists.

***September, 2007.* A scientific, social, and political bombshell.**
Publication of the pivotal book for the Darwin Anniversary Cycle, *Darwin's Lost Theory: Who We Really Are and Where We're Going.* Wholly contradicting the long embedded, economically and Bushist politically disastrous stereotype of "survival of the fittest" and "selfish gene" Darwinism, this is the widely acclaimed reconstruction of Darwin's long ignored "fully human, love and moral-action-oriented" completion for his theory of evolution. Among advance reviews by leading world scientists: "Everyone concerned with our understanding of evolution on this planet owes Loye a deep debt of gratitude": Pioneering general evolution theorist ***Ervin Laszlo.*** "In this work Loye has brought his unique erudition to an enormous and critical task, and carried it off with genius. We urgently need this book, and we need it now." Pioneering chaos theorist ***Ralph Abraham.***

October, 2007.* Riane Eisler's gripping first novel: *Dreamwalking in Havana. "A mesmerizing story of a clever child becoming her own woman, a girl discovering her sexuality, and a thinking person learning to make her way in the world of ideas" based on her own experience during the infamous Kristallnacht in Vienna. Escape from the Holocaust. Childhood growing up as a refugee from the Nazis in the sexist, racist, but also colorfully formative as well as tragic years of life for Jews in the slums and corruption of pre-Castro Cuba. Yearning for—and finally—escape to America. (See our website for new publication date).

November, 2007. **Publication of Bill Bates'** *Bates on Bush*. Internationally cherished for his cartoons of shipboard, sea port, and Carmel village life, in *Bates on Bush* Pulitzer nominee Bill Bates has become the American successor to the great Honore Daumier in the rare artistry, insight, and incisive wit of this historic exposure of the disastrous shenanigans of GWB and the Bush years.

November, 2007. **Publication of Loye's** *The Parable of the Three Villages*. A searing and soaring social vision in the genre of Orwell, James Thurber, and the best of 21st century environmental visionaries. This is the story purportedly recovered from an artifact of the ancient villages of the saintly Osanto, the vicious Snarlsgrrrr, and the woeful Mystifu. Prefiguring our own times to an amazing degree, the *Parable* tells of what happens when Snarlsgrrrr sets out to enslave and exploit the other villages with hordes of ComCon (i.e, compassionate conservative) robots.

December, 2007. **Darwin on sex, love, and the real you and me—for all ages.** Publication of the fourth book for the Darwin Anniversary Cycle, *Darwin on Love*. For the first time brought together, these are the charming, funny, scientifically meaningful but long ignored stories of the love and sex life of the wide range of animals that Darwin tells in the 95 times he writes of love in *The Descent of Man* —versus only twice for "survival of the fittest."

3,000 Years of Love

2008

***January, 2008.* Three spotlights on escalating election year concerns for the New Year.** Keyed to political, moral, and environmental concerns for America during this crucial national election year are: The first book for a new six book **Moral Evolution Cycle** for Loye, *The River and the Star: The Lost Story of the Great Explorers of the Better World.* An election-year second edition of *Bankrolling Evolution's* scientific expose of the pathology of the Bush years. An election-year second edition of *Measuring Evolution's* therapy for national and global recovery.

***February, 2008.* The perfect book for Valentine's Day gifts and readers.** Publication of the second book for the Love Cycle, *1001 Days of Love.* Prefigured in the Eisler-Loye dual biography, *3,000 Years of Love,* this is the surprising book of Valentine's Day and birthday poems written by Loye to Eisler during their thirty years together.

***April, 2008.* Spring and a vision for global moral and spiritual revolution.** Publication of the second book for the Moral Evolution Cycle, *The Glacier and the Flame I: Rediscovering Goodness.*

***May, 2008.* The perfect gift book for June weddings.** Publication of the third book for the Love Cycle, Loye's poems for Eisler during their earliest days together, *100 Days of Love.*

***July, 2008.* Still another perfect summer read—this time scandal in the book world! Thomas Wolfe, Will Durant, Jesus, Gautama, the Reverends Billy Max Featherstone, Billy Max Tillybody, and other famous and fictional figures in a saga of the nightmare world of late 20th century American publishing and politics—*Tangled Tales of the Book Trade, or the Mystery of the Missing Century,* a third book for Loye's Entertainment and Humor Cycle.

August, 2008. **Moral ammunition for the November 7 election.**
With only three months to go, publication of *The Science of Evil: What Makes Us Good or Bad?*—first of three more new books by Loye probing the moral and spiritual pathology driving both liberal and conservative concern.

September, 2008. **Scientific ammunition for the November 7 election.** With only one month to go, publication of the explosive scientific expose, fifth for the six-book Darwin Anniversary Cycle, *The Derailing of Evolution: The Story of the 100 Year Battle to Reclaim Our Lost Darwinian Future.*

October, 2008. **On target for November 7.** Publication of the third book for the Moral Evolution Cycle, *The Glacier and the Flame II: Redefining Evil.*

2009

2009. **New hope for America and Planet Earth.** Eisler's *Next Year Jerusalem.* Loye's *The Glacier and the Flame III: A Fragment of a Vision. Telling the New Story: The Place for Every One of Us in Evolution. Moral Sensitizing: A Guide to a New Method of Learning and Therapy for Teachers, Counselors, Ministers, and Self-Healers.* And a book of "bedtime stories for

3,000 Years of Love

little and big folk," *Grandfather's Garden.*

OUR AUTHORS

Initially, in addition to our focus on the work of the unusual partnership of scientist-activist-authors Eisler and Loye, we are publishing the works of award-winning, Pulitzer nominee political cartoonist Bill Bates and a prototypical goal and pace-setting philanthropist for building the better world, Robert Graham .

Riane Eisler. Riane Eisler is the internationally acclaimed thinker and author of the bestselling *The Chalice and the Blade* (an "evergreen" for booksellers, now in 22 foreign editions). In 2007 Berrett-Koehler will publish her major new book, *The Real Wealth of Nations.* The Benjamin Franklin Press will publish her first novel, *Dreamwalking in Havana.* She will co-star in the unusual Eisler-Loye dual-biography, *3,000 Years of Love.* Then in 2008 comes their haunting real life scientific mystery story, *Return to Amalfi,* and the surprise of two books of love poems by her partner David Loye

David Loye. David Loye—author of the award-winning *The Healing of a Nation,* many other books, and an internationally known evolutionary systems scientist—will publish twenty books within the almost unheard of span of only two years. An unprecedented explosion of creativity for an author in his eighties, his new books cover a startling range of fields from science, education, politics, and moral evolution, to entertainment, humor, and love.

Bill Bates. Over 36 years of cartoons Pulitzer nominee Bill Bates became a cherished icon for the artistry and wit of his poke of fun at the foibles of locals in California's tiny Carmel-by-the-Sea and thousands of travelers to seaports around the world immortalized in his work. But with the election of George W.Bush to the American presidency came the "mad as hell and not going to take it any more," 2007 California Newspaper Publishers award-winning series of cartoons for his book *Bush on Bates*—an historical statement for the annals of political cartoons likely to long endure.

Robert Graham. As an appealing exemplar for our focus on the impact of progressive money on evolution in our first two books, *Bankrolling Evolution* and *Measuring Evolution*, we're publishing *50 50 at 50: Going Just Beyond* by Robert Graham. This is Graham's inspiring tale of how, after making a fortune in canning tomatoes, he set out on the spiritual journey at age 50 that led to his formation of two foundations with top track records for improving the lives of women and families in Latin America.

FOR BOOK READERS, BUYERS, AND SELLERS

Eisler's *The Real Wealth of Nations* is published by Berrett-Koehler, available in bookstores, Amazon and other online booksellers, and through www.partnershipway.org.

Eisler's *Dreamwalking in Havana* and books by Loye, Bates, and Graham are published by the Benjamin Franklin Press. As they're printed, our books are available from online book sellers worldwide. On Amazon, Powell's, Barnes & Noble, Abe Books, and many others in the U.S. On the following websites for: Canada: amazon.ca. United Kingdom: amazon.co.uk. Germany: amazon.de. France: amazon.fr. Japan: amazon.co.jp. China (gradually): amazon.cn.

Additionally, a particularly good outlet for the United Kingdom and

3,000 Years of Love

Europe generally is the Book Depository: www.bookdepository.co.uk. And for Italy: www.ibs.it.

You can buy them in bookstores throughout the U.S. Ask for them and book stores can order through their online catalogue for the largest book distributor in America, Ingrams Book Company.

You can also purchase them through our website: www.benjaminfranklinpress.com.

For more information go to www.benjaminfranklinpress.com, or contact Elliot Sanders at the Benjamin Franklin Press, email: elliotsanders@benjaminfranklinpress.com. Phone 831-624-6037. Fax 831-626-3734. P.O. Box 222851, Carmel, CA 93923.

www.ingramcontent.com/pod-product-compliance
Lightning Source LLC
Chambersburg PA
CBHW051422290426
44109CB00016B/1395